SCIENTISTS

INSPIRING TALES OF THE WORLD'S BRIGHTEST SCIENTIFIC MINDS

Written by Isabel Thomas
Illustrated by Jessamy Hawke

CONTENTS

Incredible Chemistry

DK | Penguin Random House

Author Isabel Thomas
Illustrator Jessamy Hawke
Historical consultant Dr Stephen Haddelsey
Scientific consultant Lisa Burke

Editor Katie Lawrence
Designers Bettina Myklebust Stovne,
Brandie Tully-Scott

Additional editorial Kathleen Teece,
Sally Beets, Olivia Stanford
Publishing Coordinator Issy Walsh
Senior Picture Researcher Sumedha Chopra
Managing Editor Jonathan Melmoth
Managing Art Editor Diane Peyton Jones
Production Editor Abigail Maxwell
Senior Production Controllers Ena Matagic,
Francesca Sturiale
Publishing Director Sarah Larter

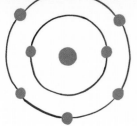

Fantastic Physics

Amazing Earth & Space

First published in Great Britain in 2021 by
Dorling Kindersley Limited
DK, One Embassy Gardens, 8 Viaduct Gardens,
London, SW11 7BW

The authorised representative in the EEA is
Dorling Kindersley Verlag GmbH. Arnulfstr. 124,
80636 Munich, Germany

Copyright © 2021 Dorling Kindersley Limited
Text copyright © Isabel Thomas, 2021
A Penguin Random House Company
10 9 8 7 6 5 4 3 2 1
001-322924-Aug/2021

A CIP catalogue record for this book
is available from the British Library.
ISBN: 978-0-2414-8433-3

Printed and bound in China

For the curious
www.dk.com

This book was made with Forest Stewardship
Council ™ certified paper - one small step in
DK's commitment to a sustainable future.

For more information go to
www.dk.com/our-green-pledge

FOREWORD

by Isabel Thomas

Imagine spending *every* day finding out more about your favourite topic in the world. This sounds too good to be true — but it's exactly what scientists do. They explore, experiment with, and try to explain the things they are most interested in, whether it's diamonds or dinosaurs, pandas or planets, volcanoes or vaccinations.

Scientists don't start from scratch, but build on previous ideas and discoveries. Isaac Newton described this as "standing on the shoulders of giants". This means that science never stands still. Over time, even the most famous, world-changing ideas are refined or replaced with better ones. Being a brilliant scientist isn't about being the brainiest person in the room, it's about curiosity, teamwork, and challenging old ideas.

In this book you'll read tales of incredible breakthroughs and ingenious discoveries — but you'll also learn that scientists themselves are really people just like you. People who love fun and friendships. People who sometimes face unfair treatment and overcome unexpected obstacles. People who don't have all the answers — only questions.

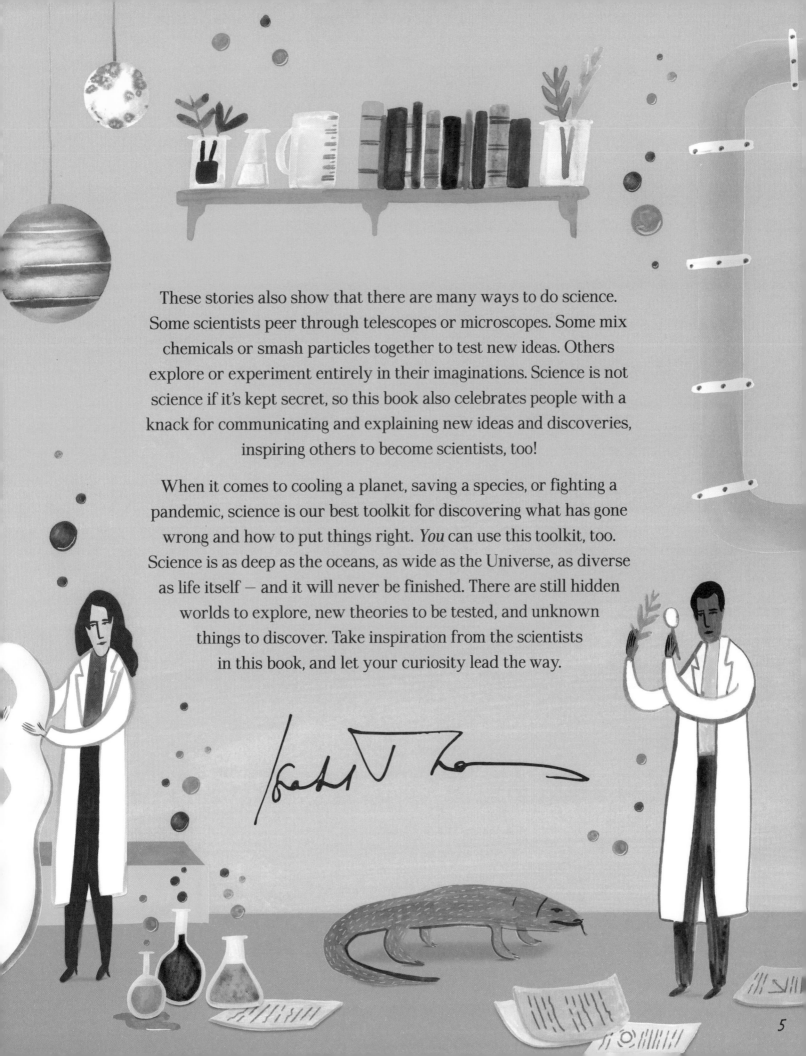

These stories also show that there are many ways to do science. Some scientists peer through telescopes or microscopes. Some mix chemicals or smash particles together to test new ideas. Others explore or experiment entirely in their imaginations. Science is not science if it's kept secret, so this book also celebrates people with a knack for communicating and explaining new ideas and discoveries, inspiring others to become scientists, too!

When it comes to cooling a planet, saving a species, or fighting a pandemic, science is our best toolkit for discovering what has gone wrong and how to put things right. *You* can use this toolkit, too. Science is as deep as the oceans, as wide as the Universe, as diverse as life itself — and it will never be finished. There are still hidden worlds to explore, new theories to be tested, and unknown things to discover. Take inspiration from the scientists in this book, and let your curiosity lead the way.

BRILLIANT BIOLOGY

Living things include the most amazing and complex structures in the known Universe. Biology is the study of life, from the tiniest microbes to the mightiest plants and animals. Biologists seek to understand living things – how they live and work together and why they succeed and fail.

MARIA SIBYLLA MERIAN

German—born naturalist and artist • 1647–1717

Maria grew up more than 300 years ago, when the lives of insects were a mystery. Most people believed that creepy-crawlies formed from dirt and rotting waste. They weren't keen to get a closer look! However, 13-year-old Maria was fearless. She roamed gardens collecting caterpillars, which she kept in a crate and watched closely. As they chomped on mulberry leaves and lettuce, Maria was amazed to see the caterpillars fatten up, form cocoons, and finally transform into fluttering silk moths.

Over 50 years, Maria repeated this experiment with hundreds of different insects. She sketched every stage and combined them to create beautiful paintings that showed the transformations. These were some of the very first drawings of the life cycles we learn about today.

Maria noticed tiny details, such as the dusty scales on a butterfly's wings.

Maria painted the plants that insects eat and the battles for survival in nature.

8

From caterpillar...

...to chrysalis...

...to butterfly!

A new view of nature

The transformation of a caterpillar to a butterfly was just one of the natural processes that Maria noticed. She didn't paint insects like they were in museums. Her creatures were full of life — growing, changing, and interacting with plants.

Trip to the tropics

Maria became well known for her paintings of European caterpillars. After moving to the Netherlands, she was invited to see huge collections of tropical insects. However, the beautiful creatures had been dried out and pinned to boards. Maria longed to see them crawling, eating, breeding, and flying around. After years of hard work and planning, she set off on her very own scientific expedition — to Suriname, in South America.

In hot, humid Suriname, local people who knew the rainforest well helped Maria to row through waters full of snapping, alligator-like creatures called caiman, to discover spectacular animals. For two years, she marvelled at spiders, snakes, and jewel-like insects. Back in the Netherlands, Maria turned her notes and sketches into a wonderful book — *Transformations of the Insects of Surinam*. Her work delighted kings and queens, and was studied by naturalists for centuries. But, perhaps Maria would be most pleased to know about the creatures named after her — a lizard, a spider, two beetles, and nine butterflies.

This species of lizard, Salvator merianae, is named after Maria.

MARY ANNING

English palaeontologist
1799–1847

In the 1800s, fossils were big business. Museums and collectors paid handsomely for the remains of long-dead plants and animals that had been frozen in time, and palaeontologist Mary Anning had a knack for finding them. Mary was born in Lyme Regis, Dorset, UK, which is one of the best places in the world to find fossils. Her father collected fossils for fun and taught his children how to find them. When he died, selling these ancient wonders became the family's only source of money.

In 1811, Mary's brother spotted the most incredible fossil they'd ever seen — an enormous skull sticking out of a cliff. Slowly and carefully, 12-year-old Mary dug the whole skeleton out of the rock. This skeleton would soon be known by the name *Ichthyosaurus*. Her career as a world-famous fossil hunter had begun.

Fossils are rocks that show us the shape of ancient and extinct plants and animals.

The plesiosaur looked so strange that at first, other palaeontologists thought it was fake!

Mary's plesiosaur is still on display at the Natural History Museum in London, UK.

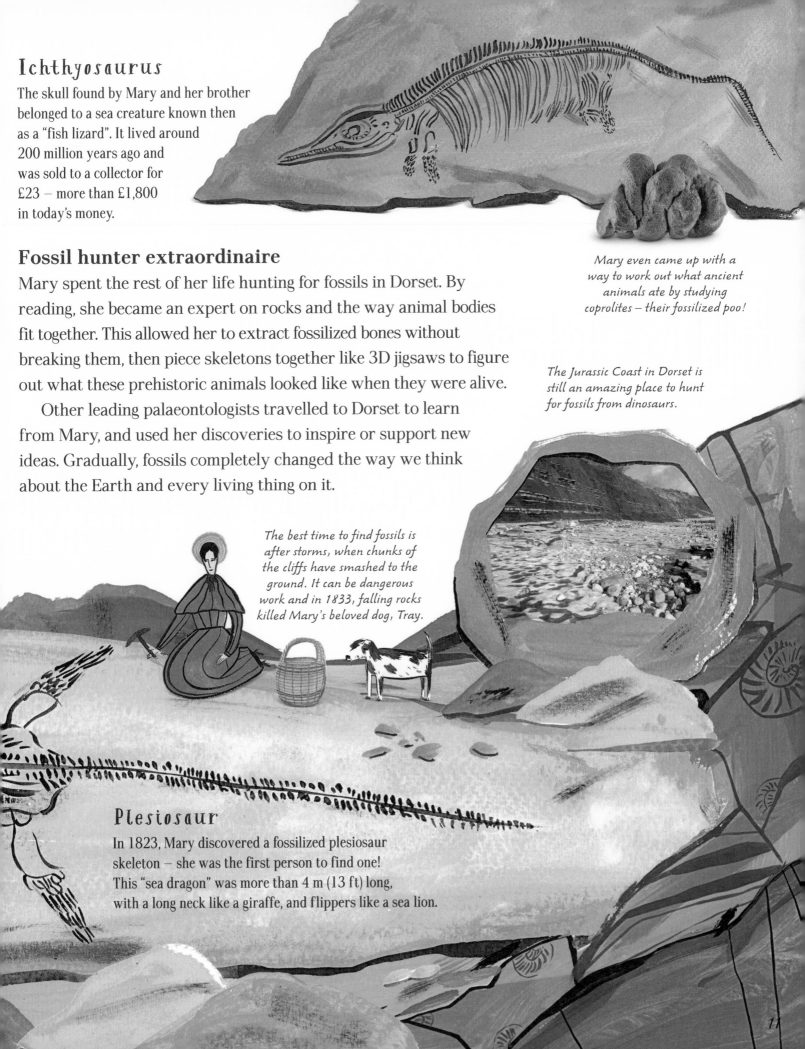

Ichthyosaurus

The skull found by Mary and her brother belonged to a sea creature known then as a "fish lizard". It lived around 200 million years ago and was sold to a collector for £23 – more than £1,800 in today's money.

Mary even came up with a way to work out what ancient animals ate by studying coprolites – their fossilized poo!

Fossil hunter extraordinaire

Mary spent the rest of her life hunting for fossils in Dorset. By reading, she became an expert on rocks and the way animal bodies fit together. This allowed her to extract fossilized bones without breaking them, then piece skeletons together like 3D jigsaws to figure out what these prehistoric animals looked like when they were alive.

Other leading palaeontologists travelled to Dorset to learn from Mary, and used her discoveries to inspire or support new ideas. Gradually, fossils completely changed the way we think about the Earth and every living thing on it.

The Jurassic Coast in Dorset is still an amazing place to hunt for fossils from dinosaurs.

The best time to find fossils is after storms, when chunks of the cliffs have smashed to the ground. It can be dangerous work and in 1833, falling rocks killed Mary's beloved dog, Tray.

Plesiosaur

In 1823, Mary discovered a fossilized plesiosaur skeleton – she was the first person to find one! This "sea dragon" was more than 4 m (13 ft) long, with a long neck like a giraffe, and flippers like a sea lion.

GREGOR MENDEL
Czech geneticist
1822–1884

Gregor Mendel grew up on a farm in the Austrian Empire (now the Czech Republic), but after studying philosophy and physics at university, he decided not to become a farmer himself. Instead, he joined a monastery to train as a monk. This gave him the chance to study more science and mathematics, too. At the monastery he worked hard teaching school students, and ran experiments in the monastery gardens. Eventually he became abbot — the person who runs the whole monastery — and he had no spare time for his plants, but he had already made an important discovery.

Secrets of life

Gregor was interested in trying to understand how certain characteristics of plants passed from parents to their offspring. He decided to investigate, using his science and maths skills.

Characteristics

Gregor studied pea plants, which were easy to grow and had characteristics that were easy to tell apart, such as their seed colour.

Genetics genius

Gregor bred pairs of parent plants with different characteristics, such as purple or white flowers. When the offspring plants grew, he recorded whether each one had purple or white flowers. Learning physics had taught Gregor to repeat experiments again and again, so next he bred pairs of the offspring plants.

Over time, Gregor collected a huge amount of data, and was able to see patterns that no one else had noticed before. He worked out that some plants must carry information for **both** purple **and** white flowers, but could only pass on one of these to their offspring. He created rules to describe how these simple "hereditary factors" worked. In 1909, these factors were renamed "genes" and the science of genetics began.

In the 20th century, Mendel's work at the monastery helped other scientists to show how variation – the natural range of differences within a species – came about and was passed on.

Strong genes

When Gregor paired plants with purple flowers and plants with white flowers, the first generation of their offspring all had purple flowers.

Gene pairs

When Gregor bred new plants from the first generation offspring, plants with white flowers reappeared! The ratio was one white flower for every three purple ones.

	C	c
C	CC	Cc
c	Cc	cc

ALFRED RUSSEL WALLACE

British explorer, naturalist, and biologist • 1823–1913

You've had a world-changing idea – now what? How do you make sure that children will be learning *your* name at school in 150 years' time? Charles Darwin is famous for the theory of evolution by natural selection. But, Alfred Russel Wallace came up with the same idea at the same time. Why did history almost forget him?

Alfred's family was not rich like Charles's. Alfred left school aged 14, to start earning money for his family. He became a surveyor, then a teacher. While teaching, Alfred read about Charles's voyage on HMS *Beagle* and decided to save up enough money to travel the world himself.

THE "KING" AND THE "TWELVE WIRED" BIRDS OF PARADISE

Alfred drew many sketches, which were published in his book The Malay Archipelago.

Many of the birds Alfred collected were new to the world of science.

This is Wallace's flying frog, which was introduced to scientists by Alfred.

Inspired by nature

Alfred made two long trips — the first was to the Amazon in South America. On his journey back from the Amazon, the ship caught fire and, tragically, Alfred lost almost all of the specimens he had collected. However, he was not discouraged and in 1854, Alfred set off on another expedition to the Malay Archipelago (modern-day Malaysia and Indonesia). Here, he built up an enormous collection of almost 126,000 specimens of plants, animals, and insects.

Alfred started thinking about why there are so many different types of animals, and how they change, or evolve, over time. He was resting in bed with a fever one day when he came up with the answer: natural selection.

Natural selection

Most plants and animals have more offspring than can possibly survive. These offspring are not identical — their features vary. The ones with features best suited to their habitat are more likely to survive and go on to have offspring themselves. The features that helped them survive are passed on. Alfred realized that when you put these facts together, it explains how species change, or adapt, over time.

Charles Darwin

Alfred knew that another naturalist called Charles Darwin (1809–1882) was also interested in evolution. He wrote him a letter explaining his idea. When Charles got the letter, he was shocked to read about the same idea he had been working on for almost 20 years!

What happened next?

1858
Charles shares the theory of natural selection with other scientists, giving Alfred credit, too. Alfred is still travelling, so he finds out later.

1859
Charles finishes his huge book about natural selection, On the Origin of Species. It gets lots of attention.

1862
Alfred returns to the UK. He supports Charles, and begins writing his own books, including The Malay Archipelago.

1860s–1870s
Charles and Alfred battle to win support for their theory. Most people use the name "Darwinism" to describe it, but Alfred doesn't mind — he is Charles's biggest supporter!

1930s–1940s
Biologists become interested in natural selection again. Charles's book, full of evidence, is the focus. His name becomes well-known once again.

NETTIE STEVENS

American geneticist
1861–1912

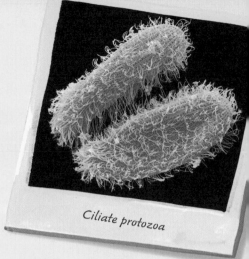

Ciliate protozoa

The first creatures Nettie studied were protozoa, which are made up of just one cell.

From beetles to blue whales, most animals have two sexes: male and female. With two sexes, animals can take part in a process called reproduction. Female animals make special cells, called gametes, with half of the instructions needed for a new baby animal. Male animals make gametes that contain the other half of the instructions. When these two sets of instructions join together in an egg cell — in a process called fertilization — the cell starts to develop into a new baby animal.

But why do some eggs develop into female animals, while others develop into males? Is it to do with the conditions they grow in, such as the temperature or food supply? Or is it something inside the cells themselves? Nettie Stevens was the first scientist to answer this question.

After protozoa, Nettie studied the gametes and fertilized eggs of mealworm beetles.

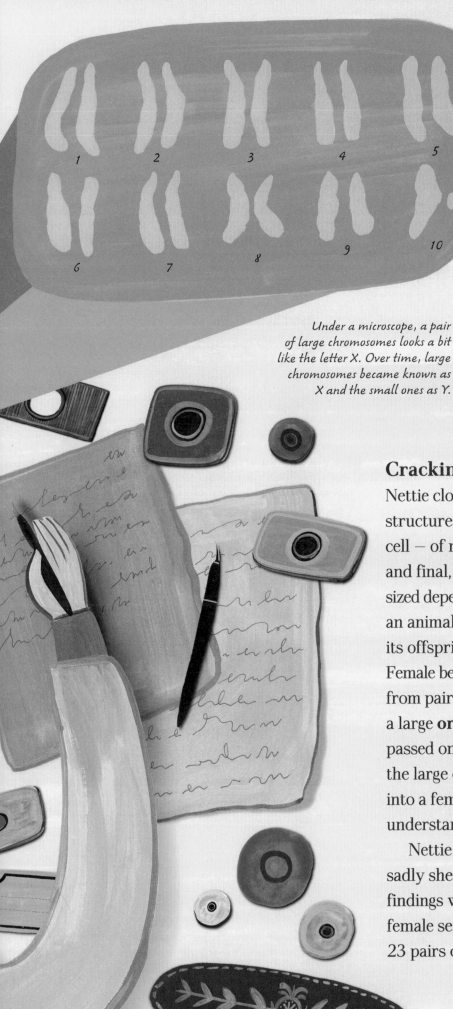

Mealworm chromosomes

Using a microscope, Nettie looked closely at mealworm chromosomes. Mealworm beetles have 20 chromosomes, arranged into 10 pairs. Nettie noticed that cells from female beetles each contain 20 large chromosomes. But, cells from male beetles contain 19 large chromosomes and 1 small one.

Under a microscope, a pair of large chromosomes looks a bit like the letter X. Over time, large chromosomes became known as X and the small ones as Y.

Cracking chromosomes

Nettie closely studied chromosomes — tiny structures that contain the instructions for each cell — of mealworms. She realized that the tenth, and final, pair of chromosomes was unequally sized depending on the sex of the beetle. Remember: an animal can only pass half of its instructions to its offspring — one chromosome from each pair. Female beetles can only pass on large chromosomes from pair 10. But, male beetles may pass on either a large **or** a small chromosome. If the small one is passed on, the egg will develop into a male, and if the large one is passed on, the egg will develop into a female. This was a huge breakthrough in understanding how cells work.

Nettie published her research in 1905, but sadly she died before it was proven that her findings were typical of all animals with male and female sexes. This includes humans, who have 23 pairs of chromosomes.

GEORGE WASHINGTON CARVER

American agricultural chemist, agronomist, and inventor • 1860s–1943

George Washington Carver was born into slavery. This means that his family were treated as if they were the property of the farm where they lived. They were forced to work for no pay and were not free to leave.

Slavery was banned in the USA when George was a few years old, but he continued to live on the farm. He loved gardening, and he even began experimenting with ways to improve the soil and keep crop-eating pests away. George left the farm when he was about 12 years old, but at that time it was impossible for an African-American student to get a place at a high school or college.

George created more than 300 different peanut products, such as flour, oil, plastics, and soap.

Peanut oil

Peanut flour

Soil science

George worked in different jobs until his late 20s, when he earned a place at an agricultural college to study plant science. George quickly won a reputation as a fantastic scientist. In 1896, he was invited to join the Tuskegee Institute in Alabama to carry out his own research. George liked science because it gave him a way to help people. He started looking for ways to improve life for farming families, many of whom had once been enslaved themselves.

There's a crater on the Moon named in George's honour.

George travelled around to share his knowledge with farmers and teach them new techniques. He used a wagon as his classroom.

At first farmers didn't want to grow crops that they couldn't sell, such as peanuts, even if it did improve the soil. But, by 1915, George's crop rotation methods had turned the struggling farms in the south of the USA into some of the country's biggest suppliers of agricultural products. Peanuts were now one of the most important crops grown in the USA.

Crop rotation

Cotton was the main crop grown in the south of the USA. However, it used up all the nutrients in the soil, and fertilizer that helped the soil recover was expensive. George experimented with crop rotation, which means planting different crops each year. He discovered that growing peanuts, soybeans, and sweet potatoes helped soil to recover lost nutrients.

George found new ways to use sweet potatoes other than just as food. He worked out that parts of the plant could be used to make fabric, rope, rubber, and glue!

19

As a child, Joan Beauchamp Procter loved reptiles more than books, other pets, and even birthday presents! She longed to study zoology at university, but suffered from frequent illness that made this seem impossible. However, Joan had been writing to the chief herpetologist (person who studies reptiles and amphibians) at the British Museum in the UK. He was so impressed by Joan's knowledge and enthusiasm of reptiles that he offered her a job at the museum when she left school. There, Joan created displays and illustrated postcards. She also began to help to design the homes of animals at London Zoo, and in 1923, she was offered her dream job — curator, or manager, of the zoo's Reptile House.

Joan wrote her first scientific paper aged 19, about a dangerous snake called a pit viper.

Joan became famous around the world for her reptile knowledge. Her most well-known scientific paper shared her discoveries about the pancake tortoise.

Joan was said to keep a pet crocodile in her bathtub, but it was probably just a lizard.

JOAN BEAUCHAMP PROCTER

British zoologist • 1897–1931

The roof and walls of the Reptile House were made from glass to let in sunlight, which is important to keep reptiles healthy.

Creature comforts

Joan set to work creating the best reptile house in the world. To do that, she needed to combine all of her knowledge about how reptile bodies work and the kinds of places they lived in the wild. She added "furniture" that imitated jungle habitats, with caves, real trees, and swimming pools. She had cacti sent over from the USA to make desert snakes feel at home. And to stop mould growing, the walls were covered in car paint, which was easy to clean, too.

When the new Reptile House opened in 1927, it was a huge success. The reptiles moved around more, grew bigger, and lived longer, happier lives here. Joan's excellent enclosure is still being used today.

Reptile thermoregulation

Joan understood that reptiles cannot make their own body heat. They must bask in sunlight to warm up and sit in shade to cool down. Joan installed human-made sun lamps and heated rocks to help the reptiles control their temperature. This kept the reptiles healthy, and cleverly encouraged them to sit where visitors could admire them.

Joan's biggest honour was having two reptile species named after her: the snake Buhoma procterae, and the tortoise Testudo procterae.

Joan was comfortable around even the largest reptiles, such as the fearsome Komodo dragon.

Towards the end of her time at the zoo, Joan could only travel around the grounds in a wheelchair, because she was so poorly.

RACHEL CARSON

American biologist, writer, and ecologist • 1907–1964

Rachel Carson described her job as "poet of the sea". She explored the seashore with all of her senses, and wrote at length about her own experiences so that everyone could feel the soft mist, smell the salty air, hear the rushing waves, and watch swooping seabirds through her eyes.

Rachel grew up on a farm far from the ocean, and always wanted to be a writer. As a teenager she saw the ocean for the first time, and knew she had to be a biologist, too. She dreamed of studying ecosystems — communities of plants and animals living in a specific area — and learning about nature.

Wildlife [...] is dwindling because its home is being destroyed, but the home of the wildlife is also our home.

Lobster

Periwinkle

A natural writer

Rachel combined her biology education with her love for writing and nature. As a wildlife editor for the government, she wrote radio programmes about sea life. She also wrote many magazine articles and books of her own. These used a very different style of writing to other science books, blending poetic language and science in a way that made people care deeply about the natural world.

Rachel's research and books show how humans are also a part of nature. They tell of how science has helped us to discover the wonders of nature, but also warn of the damage humans can do to ecosystems. Rachel's work changed attitudes so much, that it led to new laws, and even a brand-new government agency tasked with protecting the environment.

Her book Silent Spring *made people realize that it is important to look after the environment.*

Rachel's first books focused on the seashore, the part of nature she loved the best. Her book The Sea Around Us *was made into an award-winning film.*

DDT damage
Rachel was worried about the use of strong chemicals, such as dichlorodiphenyltrichloroethane (DDT for short!), to kill insect pests. These chemicals were also bad for other wildlife. Rachel helped to alert the world to the dangers of DDT, and eight years after she died, it was banned in the USA.

Ibis bird eggs damaged by DDT

As a trainee scientist, Rachel studied the life of catfish.

Catfish

American eel

23

SABIHA KASIMATI

Albanian ichthyologist • 1912–1951

Black sea bream

Rudd

Corfu toothcarp

Flounder

Scientists don't just spend all day thinking about science! They make a difference in other areas of life, too. Sabiha Kasimati is famous for being Albania's first female scientist, and first ichthyologist (fish scientist). However, she is also celebrated for standing up for reason and science, when they were under attack.

Sabiha grew up in Turkey and Albania. She learned to speak many languages, and studied biology in Italy. Afterwards, she returned to Albania to work in the National Institute of Sciences. For 10 years, Sabiha found out everything she could about the fish living in Albania's ponds, rivers, lakes, and coastal lagoons. But, she had to be careful about everything she did and said — Albania was ruled by Enver Hoxha, a dictator (ruler with total power) who was using force to get his own way. People who upset him were being imprisoned, sent away, or even executed.

Adriatic sturgeon

Fishing was important in Albania, but no scientist had really studied the country's fish before. Sabiha visited all kinds of places to collect specimens. She identified them, sorted them into groups, mapped their habitats, and learned about their life cycles.

Peacock gudgeon

Centre of research

In 1948, Sabiha had the idea of setting up Albania's Museum of Natural Sciences. It is now named after her. It's not only a museum, but a centre of research into the variety of Albanian animals, including fish.

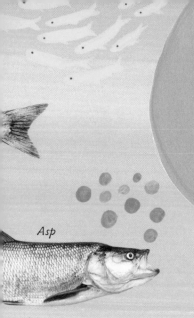

Asp

Act of bravery

It was a particularly dangerous time to be a scientist, because scientists are people who look for evidence and notice when lies are being told. Sabiha was horrified to hear that one of her old science teachers had been sentenced to death because he had opposed Enver's new rules. Sabiha had met Enver before, when they were in the same class at school, and she bravely arranged to meet him. Sabiha argued that what Enver was doing was wrong.

Adriatic trout

Black bullhead

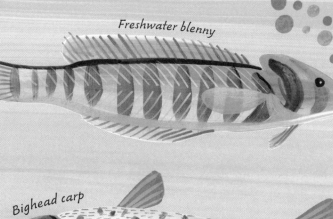

Freshwater blenny

Bighead carp

Not long afterwards, Sabiha was arrested and accused of a crime she didn't commit. Tragically, Sabiha didn't get a chance to defend herself in court – she was one of a group of people killed without a trial.

Rainbow trout

ROSALIND FRANKLIN

English chemist
1920–1958

In the mid-20th century, several teams of scientists were competing to understand a mysterious molecule called deoxyribonucleic acid (DNA). This is found in the cells of every living thing. The scientists knew that DNA carried the instructions for building living things, but no one knew how it worked!

Rosalind Franklin was an expert at taking photographs of tiny molecules and using these pictures to work out what they were made from. In May 1952, she took her best photo yet, showing that DNA was shaped like a twisted ladder. Rosalind had found a key piece of the puzzle — one that other scientists would use to make the all-important discovery about the structure of DNA.

DNA's twisted-ladder shape is known as the double helix.

X-ray crystallography

Rosalind didn't take her photographs using an ordinary camera. She did it by passing X-rays through crystals of a molecule and looking closely at the shadowy patterns they made. The patterns revealed how atoms are arranged inside the molecules.

FRANCIS CRICK & JAMES WATSON

English
molecular biologist
1916–2004

American
molecular biologist
1928–present

In a laboratory in Cambridge, UK, Francis Crick and James Watson had also been racing to understand the structure of DNA. Rather than trying to photograph the molecule, they carried out tests to find which chemicals DNA was made from. Then, they made models to try to work out how these chemicals fitted together — like giant, complicated, 3D jigsaw puzzles!

In 1953, a scientist from Rosalind's laboratory showed Rosalind's photo of DNA to James. He raced back to the lab so that he and Francis could build 3D models of a double helix. All the different chemicals in DNA could finally be fitted together, thanks to the work of Rosalind, Francis, and James.

The secret of life

The discovery made by Rosalind, Francis, and James helped us work out how DNA carries instructions for all the proteins that build a living thing. Learning to read this code has allowed us to use science in new ways, such as to catch criminals, defeat viruses, and save more lives with medicine.

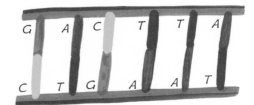

A coded sequence of DNA is made up of four chemicals — Adenine (A), Thymine (T), Guanine (G), and Cytosine (C). A always pairs up with T, and G always pairs up with C.

27

THE CODE OF LIFE

The science of DNA is a long story, featuring thousands of plants, animals, people, and microbes. Here are some of the key stepping stones in the quest to read, to understand, and even to change the molecule that codes all life on Earth.

Double helix

Rosalind's image helps James Watson and Francis Crick to work out the structure of DNA – a double helix. This is a big clue to how it works.

Marshall Nirenberg, Har Khorana, and Severo Ochoa decipher the code inside DNA – it instructs cells to build proteins.

Scientists develop ways to read the order of chemicals called nucleotides inside DNA – this is called sequencing.

1953

1966

1975/77

A disease called sickle cell anaemia is shown to be caused by an abnormal gene that can be passed from parent to child.

1978

Gene transfer

Scientists work out how to take a gene from one living thing and add it to the DNA of a mouse or a fruit fly. A gene is a stretch of DNA that tells a cell how to make a certain protein.

Insulin is manufactured by adding the gene that makes it to bacteria, turning the bacteria into tiny insulin factories! Insulin can treat a disease called diabetes.

PCR

A method for making millions of copies of a stretch of DNA is developed, called a polymerase chain reaction (PCR). It makes it much easier to sequence DNA, and to work out what genes do.

1983

1981

1982

2020

Rapid genome sequencing helps scientists understand the coronavirus that causes COVID-19. CRISPR gene-editing technology is used to help develop vaccines.

2020

CRISPR therapies

The gene editing therapy used for sickle cell disease – clustered regularly interspaced short palindromic repeats (CRISPR) – is used inside other patients' bodies. It treats illnesses that affect the eyes and liver.

Gregor Mendel realizes that characteristics (features) of living things are passed on from their parents, in units later called genes.

1866

Friedrich Miescher finds a molecule in the nucleus of pus cells, and calls it "nuclein".

1869

Walter Flemming sees structures inside cells, called chromosomes, double before the cell divides, so each new cell gets one copy.

1879

Albrecht Kossel works out which molecule makes nuclein, and names it deoxyribonucleic acid – or DNA for short.

1881

Basics of genetics

Using cells from maize (corn) plants, Harriet Creighton and Barbara McClintock show that chromosomes carry genetic information.

1931

Rosalind Franklin takes the clearest photograph of DNA yet.

1951

Oswald Avery, Colin MacLeod, and Maclyn McCarty prove that DNA is not just a building block of chromosomes – it also carries genetic information.

1944

A photograph of DNA is produced, showing it has a regular structure.

1943

Changing genes

Scientists begin to work on a tool for editing genes. It takes 30 years to develop, but today, scientists can change DNA and the way that genes function.

DNA sequencing

Projects begin to sequence the entire human genome – that's all of our genetic material. It took more than 10 years to read the 3 billion letters in the human DNA code. Today's technology allows anyone's genome to be read accurately.

Genetically modified foods

Tomatoes are the first genetically modified crops to go on sale. Today, gene editing is widely used to give crops useful traits, such as the ability to fend off mould.

1987

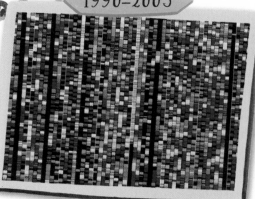

1990–2003

1994

40 years after sickle cell disease was shown to be genetic, gene editing therapy is first used to treat the condition.

2019

DNA from 40,000-year-old Neanderthal bones is studied to find out more about how these prehistoric people are related to modern humans.

2010

Scientists begin sequencing the genomes of microbes that live in and on our bodies, to better understand their role in health and disease.

2008

ENDEL TULVING

Canadian-Estonian psychologist and neuroscientist
1927-present

Can you remember what you got for your last birthday? How about your first? Why is it easy to remember the meaning of every word in this sentence, but hard to recall what you ate for lunch last Tuesday? Memory is one of the most mysterious things in science.

Endel Tulving is a scientist who set out to understand it. He grew up in Europe, then moved to Canada in 1949 where he studied psychology — the science of the human mind and behaviour. This was a new science at the time and there were so many unanswered questions.

Episodic memory

Types of memory

Endel came up with a theory to explain how our brains organize long-term memories. Episodic memory lets us play back things we have seen or done ourselves, such as our last birthday party. Semantic memory stores the things we have learned and now know — such as what a dog is! Endel later added a third type of memory to his theory, procedural memory. This type stores information about how to do things, such as riding a bike.

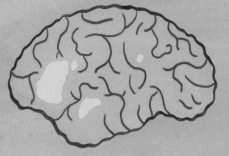

Endel used brain scans to show that different parts of the brain "light up" with activity when we store memories and when we retrieve them.

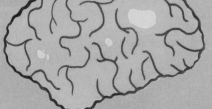

Storing a memory   *Accessing a memory*

Semantic memory

Dog

Procedural memory

Endel developed a way to use positron emission tomography (PET) scanning to see memories in action.

A single human brain may be able to store a quadrillion bytes of data – as much information as is on the entire Internet!

Making memories

How do people store words, facts, skills, and memories, and recall them exactly when needed? Endel designed experiments to find out more. One of his experiments involved 900 school students. It showed that different parts of the brain are involved in storing and retrieving memories. Both processes are needed for us to remember something. Next, Endel explored memories themselves and defined three different types.

Studying the mind is very difficult. We cannot see a brain from the outside, and it's dangerous to start poking around inside! As medical technology improved, Endel found ways to safely watch the brain at work. This helped him prove that different areas of the brain are involved in storing and retrieving memories.

YUAN LONGPING

Chinese agronomist
1930–present

After studying soil and crop science at university, Yuan Longping became a teacher and researcher at a farming college. At first his research focused on sweet potatoes. However, when a terrible famine in China left millions of people without food, Longping switched to studying rice – the main plant food eaten in China. In 1961, Longping came across a rice plant that had plumper grains than usual. If there were more plants like this, he thought, then more people could be fed.

However, Longping knew that the plant's seeds might not grow into plants with the same large grains. He needed to be sure that this characteristic was passed on. Longping came up with a plan to breed the plant with other rice plants that had useful characteristics. This way, the seeds would gain the best characteristics from both parents.

China has around 20 per cent of the world's population, but only nine per cent of the world's land on which to grow crops.

Hybrid rice was born

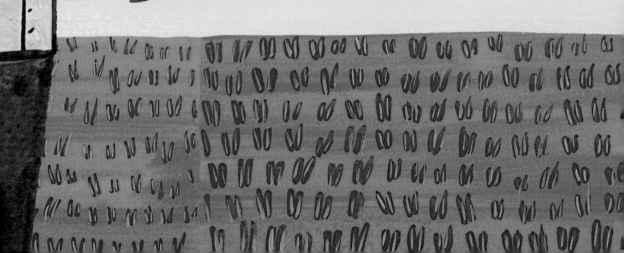

A recipe for super rice

Seeds for new plants are formed when pollen meets an egg. Longping knew that farmed rice plants usually pollinated themselves, making it difficult to breed them with other rice plants. However, in 1970, he came across some wild rice that had eggs and no pollen. It was perfect for what he needed.

By 1973, Longping had bred the wild rice with the farmed rice to create a new species of super rice, which produced 20 per cent more grain than normal! He continued his work for three decades, getting better and better results. The super rice helped to ensure a steady supply of food in China, because more rice could be grown on less land. Now grown on other continents, too, the rice is helping to tackle food shortages around the world.

Farmed rice

Wild rice

Hybrid rice

Hybrid rice

When two things are combined to make something new, it's called a hybrid. Plants created from parents of two different plant varieties often grow faster and produce more seeds.

Longping is still trying to improve the super rice, helping it to capture more of the Sun's energy to grow even better.

in China, but it belongs to all.

33

DIAN FOSSEY
American primatologist
1932–1985

Wild mountain gorillas are among the world's rarest animals, living in just two areas of east-central Africa. In the 1960s, few people had ever seen a mountain gorilla up close. Films and stories, such as *King Kong*, had given these great apes a reputation for being fierce and dangerous. Dian Fossey was one of the first scientists to live alongside mountain gorillas, and her discoveries changed our ideas about apes, and humans, forever. Dian set up a small research station in the forest, high up in the Virunga Mountains in Rwanda. Here, she could watch mountain gorillas every day.

I imitated their natural, normal behaviour like feeding, munching on celery stalks or scratching myself.

Dian named the gorillas and described their different personalities. Her favourite was called Digit, after his crooked finger.

Into the wild

At first the gorillas were shy, but as Dian lived with them and copied their behaviour, she won their trust. This process, known as habituation, meant that Dian could now watch the gorillas acting naturally. She began to understand how they live in close-knit family groups and spend much of their time eating plants.

Battle for survival

However, life was neither easy nor peaceful. The gorillas were badly affected by human activities, such as farming, and were sometimes hunted by poachers. Dian's research inspired people around the world to care about mountain gorillas. But, as the number of mountain gorillas fell to around 250, Dian became sad and angry.

In her 18 years in the mountains, Dian fought to protect these incredible creatures. She argued with poachers and farmers, and conservationists who wanted to help the gorillas in different ways. Dian died in 1985. Other scientists and conservationists carried on the work she had started, and the gorilla population began to grow. Today, there are around 1,000 wild mountain gorillas. It's the only conservation programme that has increased numbers of a group of wild apes.

Dian's incredible life story was made into a Hollywood film – Gorillas in the Mist. Her many photographs and videos have helped people to understand gorillas much better.

The Karisoke Research Centre that Dian founded in Rwanda trains scientists, conservationists, and local communities.

35

Mayana is trying to understand and treat a neuromuscular condition called Duchenne muscular dystrophy (DMD). It's caused by a change in a gene that means the body cannot make a certain protein that keeps muscles strong.

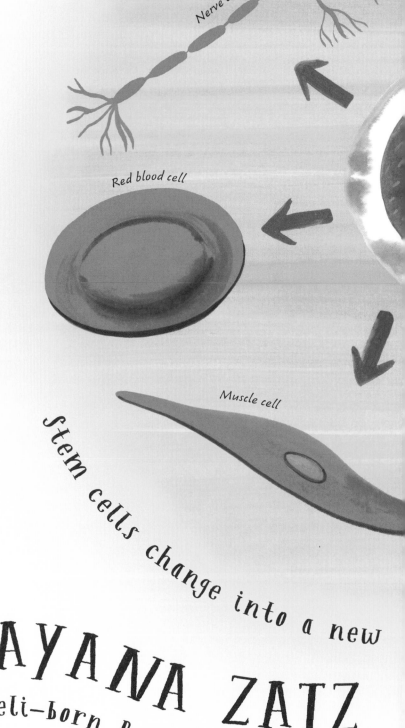

Nerve cell

Red blood cell

Muscle cell

What do you want to be when you grow up? Mayana Zatz found this impossible to answer! She wanted to be a doctor so she could help people, but also a scientist so she could learn more about why people get ill in the first place.

Mayana found a way to be both. As a specialist in human genetics, she carries out research *and* works with patients. One of her first projects was investigating the causes of neuromuscular conditions, which affect nerves and muscles.

Stem cells change into a new

MAYANA ZATZ
Israeli-born Brazilian geneticist
1947–present

36

Stem cells

Most cells in our bodies are specialized – they have a certain shape and do a specific job. Stem cells are different. They have the potential to become different types of cell, so they can be used to replace cells that are diseased, damaged, or faulty. We all have some stem cells in our bodies, but only the stem cells in an early embryo can become *any* type of cell.

This is what a three-day-old human embryo looks like under a powerful microscope. It's balanced on the point of a pin! The cells inside are stem cells.

Stem cell

Fat cell

Bone cell

type of cell permanently.

Genetic detective work

Working as part of a team, Mayana helped to identify six genes that can be passed from parents to children and may sometimes cause neuromuscular conditions. She worked closely with affected families and was shocked to find out how little support they had. Mayana founded a charity that helps children with neuromuscular conditions to access education, as well as wheelchairs and physiotherapy.

Genetics research can help us to understand infectious diseases, too. Mayana's team has been investigating the Zika virus, which is carried and passed to humans by mosquitoes.

Mayana also won funding to set up a centre for genetics research at the University of São Paulo, in Brazil. There, her team looks for new ways to treat genetic diseases – for example, by using stem cell therapies. Mayana helps politicians and the public to understand the science behind stem cells, and how these new types of treatments could be used to save millions of lives in the future.

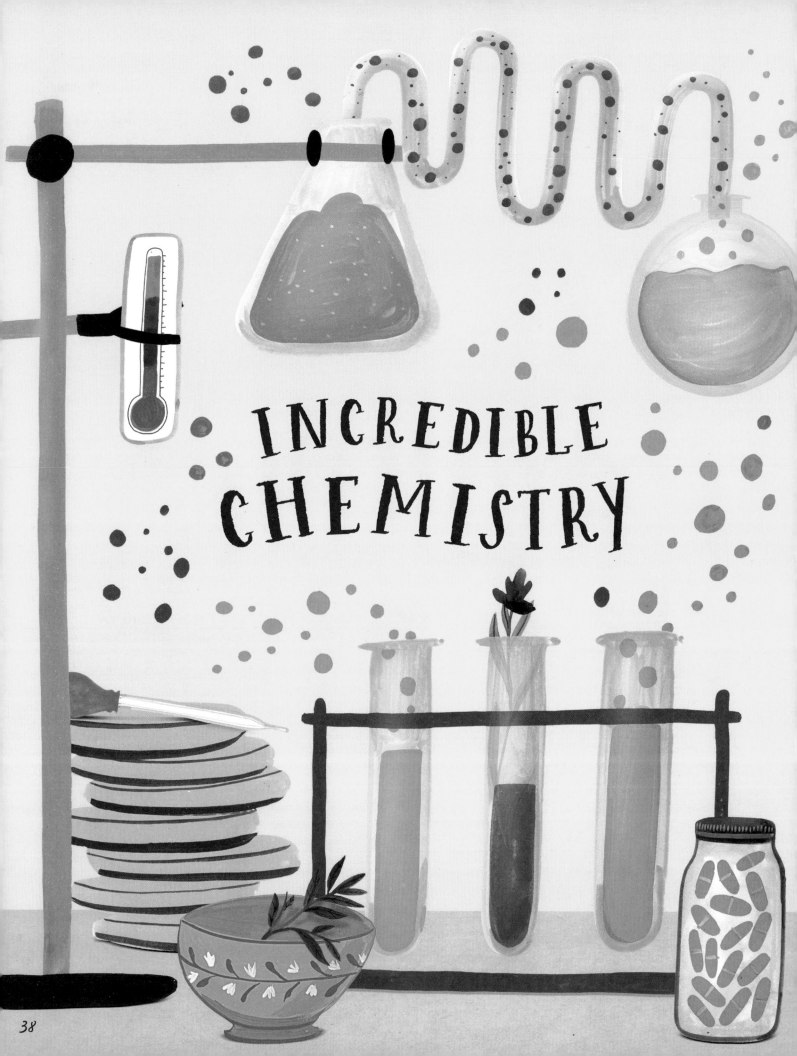

INCREDIBLE
CHEMISTRY

Chemists ask what things are made of, why substances have certain properties, and why they behave the way they do. Through chemistry, we can better understand the building blocks of everything — and seek to create brand-new substances and materials that can change the way we live.

ANTOINE LAVOISIER

French chemist • 1743–1794

Chemists study substances, asking how they behave and what they are made of. Today, we know a lot of the answers. The periodic table lists all of the building blocks of the Universe — the elements. But, when Antoine Lavoisier started his life in science, people were still arguing about what elements actually were.

Antoine began by studying air. He knew that it was involved in lots of different things, such as fire, breathing, and even the rusting of metals. At the time, many people thought that fire itself was an element, called phlogiston, which was released when a substance caught fire. Antoine set out to prove that this idea was wrong.

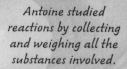

Antoine studied reactions by collecting and weighing all the substances involved.

Glass flask

Compound of mercury and oxygen

Furnace

Theory of combustion

After almost 15 years, and dozens of experiments, Antoine proved there is no such thing as phlogiston. He explained that burning is actually a fast chemical reaction between a fuel and oxygen in the air. This reaction is also known as combustion.

Chemical curiosities

Antoine's experiments showed that nothing is created or destroyed during a chemical reaction. Things are just shuffled around and changed into different forms. This is known as the "law of conservation of mass". His experiments also showed that air and water are not elements, as the ancient Greeks had believed.

Air is a mixture of different gases, including oxygen. Water is a compound — a substance made up of two building blocks: oxygen and hydrogen. Antoine's work ignited a revolution in chemistry and a race to find new elements. It also guided other chemists in how to study the world, based on careful experiments and observations.

Antoine made one of the first lists of elements — substances that cannot be broken apart into simpler parts.

Antoine referred to his early list of elements as "simple substances".

Bell jar

Water

Heating the compound released oxygen, which bubbled up into the bell jar, pushing the water out.

As a wealthy former official, Antoine was arrested during the French Revolution, when the French political system was overthrown. He was then executed by guillotine — a device built to chop off a person's head.

JEONG YAKYONG

Korean scholar, philosopher, and poet
1762–1836

Jeong Yakyong was a young man in his twenties when he became one of the most trusted advisors to the Korean ruler, King Jeongjo. At this time, new ideas from China and Europe were flooding into Korea. Jeong was brilliant at collecting and looking into the new pieces of information. He worked out how to combine them with traditional ideas. Like the king, Jeong wanted to use science and technology to improve how Korea was run. He worked closely with the king to plan changes to the country.

Jeong Yakyong is also known as "Dasan".

Today, Hwaseong Fortress is protected and celebrated as an UNESCO World Heritage site.

At the age of 31, Jeong was put in charge of the construction of a new fortress for Korea's capital city. He used the best ideas, and new technology such as complex cranes, to design a fort that was both beautiful and brilliantly designed to keep out attackers.

In a world before computers, Jeong used writing to record other people's ideas and to come up with new ones. He wrote almost 2,500 poems and more than 500 books, on a huge range of topics – from politics and science, to music and medicine.

Excelling in exile

Disaster struck when King Jeongjo died in 1800. The new Queen Regent used Jeong's interest in outside ideas as an excuse to banish him from the royal palace. For 18 years, Jeong lived in exile in a tiny, cramped room, but he didn't stop studying and writing. In fact, he worked harder than ever! He was especially interested in finding ways to tackle poverty and help the poorest Koreans, including farmers. Today's scientists are still learning from Jeong's approach to data, and how he used it to solve big, practical problems.

Jeong wanted to pass his ideas on to others. He built a pavilion near the sea for teaching students, and for sharing tea!

Fresh tea leaves → Dried tea leaves → Ground tea leaves → Compressed tea leaves

In exile, Jeong brewed tea outdoors on top of a flat rock. He experimented with different ways of preparing the leaves. One of his favourite methods was to squash them into a solid lump, to be mixed with boiling water.

"Dasan" means "mountain of tea".

Terrific tea

Jeong was interested in the science of tea, and believed that it improved his health. He also learned about the cultural traditions and rituals for preparing and tasting it. He worked closely with local Buddhists on a plan to plant new tea trees in south-west Korea.

EDWARD JENNER
English doctor and chemist
1749–1823

The hunt for a coronavirus vaccination became headline news in 2020, but the story of this important method of disease prevention began more than 200 years ago. As a doctor in the 18th century, Edward Jenner often saw patients with a terrible disease called smallpox. He noticed a pattern: farm workers who had recovered from a similar, yet milder, disease called cowpox seemed to be protected from smallpox.

Edward tested this theory by infecting a nine-year-old boy with cowpox on purpose. Two months later, he dabbed the child with pus from a smallpox patient, but the boy didn't get ill. Edward called his new treatment "vaccination" after the Latin word for cow: *vacca*. Edward's discovery was very successful and saved millions of lives. Eventually, by 1980, the disease was eradicated — there are no more smallpox cases anywhere in the world.

Smallpox

Smallpox had been a dreaded disease for thousands of years. Edward's cowpox vaccinations made it possible to prevent it. It was an amazing discovery given that at the time, no one knew what viruses were, or how immune systems worked! Before the vaccinations, 3 out of every 10 people who caught smallpox died, and survivors were often left with terrible scars.

Smallpox virus

Cowpox blisters

As a patient's body learned to fight the cowpox virus, it also learned to fight the similar smallpox virus.

LOUIS PASTEUR
French biologist and chemist
1822–1895

Scientists wanted to use Edward's ideas to protect people against other diseases, but it wasn't that easy. Other diseases didn't have milder forms like smallpox, so it would take a new technique to create vaccinations for them. Louis Pasteur figured out how to do just that.

Louis' work began with his discovery that microbes (tiny living things) were responsible for spoiling wine. He worked out that by gently heating the wine, he would kill any harmful microbes in it. This process is called "pasteurization" and is still used to help milk, fruit juice, and other foods last longer on supermarket shelves.

Microbe magician

After Louis found that heating deadly microbes made them weaker, he injected them into animals. The microbes weren't strong enough to make the animals ill, but their immune systems learned how to recognize and fight the invaders. If one of the animals came across the same microbes in the future, its immune system destroyed them. Although this new technique had nothing to do with cowpox, Louis kept the name vaccination in honour of Edward.

Vaccinations

Today, vaccinations are still made using dead or weakened microbes. Dozens of diseases that were once common and deadly can now be controlled and prevented, such as tetanus, measles, and polio. This saves millions of lives every year.

Louis' pasteurization process

Heat applied   Let flask sit   No microbes present

DMITRI MENDELEEV

Russian chemist • 1834–1907

Be
Beryllium

17
Cl
Chlorine

Dmitri Mendeleev was the brains behind one of the most important tools used by chemists and materials scientists all over the world — the periodic table. He was the youngest of 14 siblings, and life was hard for the family, especially when their father died. However, Dmitri's mother noticed his brilliant mind and was determined to give him a good science education. In 1849, she walked with him across Russia, to help him find a place at university.

Dmitri finished top of his class, then became a chemist and teacher. It was an exciting time to be a scientist — chemistry was changing so fast that Dmitri had to write his own textbook!

Dmitri arranged elements in different ways to try and spot patterns.

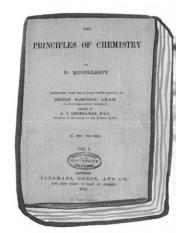

The Principles of Chemistry — *Dmitri's chemistry textbook*

Li	Be	B	C	N	O	F
Na	Mg	Al	Si	P	S	Cl
K	Ca		Ti	V	Cr	Mn	Fe, Co, Ni, Cu
(Cu)	Zn		As	Se	Br
Rb	Sr	Yt	Zr	Nb	Mo		Ru, Rh, Pd, Ag

He left gaps for unknown elements!

H

Sb

Cd **Au**

On the trip from Siberia to Moscow, and then St. Petersburg, Dmitri and his mother walked more than 1,600 km (994 miles)!

Gallium was discovered by French chemist Paul-Émile Lecoq de Boisbaudran.

Predicting elements

From the gaps in his table, Dmitri was able to predict what undiscovered elements would be like. When the element gallium was discovered, he was proved right. It's a strange metal that is solid at room temperature but melts in your hands!

Elemental jigsaw puzzle

During the 1800s, dozens of new chemical elements — the building blocks of everything — were discovered. Dmitri collected information about each known element, such as the weight of their atoms, and tried to spot patterns. He noticed that elements of very different atomic weight could be similar in other ways.

Dmitri made a chart that showed this pattern, leaving gaps where he thought new elements might be discovered. The elements were arranged in order of atomic weight, starting with the lightest. But he placed them in rows, or periods, so that elements with similar properties, such as metals, lined up to form groups. Today's periodic table of the elements looks different from Dmitri's first chart, but it's based on the same ingenious ideas. It is one of the most important tools in chemistry.

The modern periodic table shows all 118 known elements.

By smashing atoms together, physicists have been able to create elements that don't exist in nature. One was named Mendelevium, in honour of Dmitri.

101
Md
Mendelevium

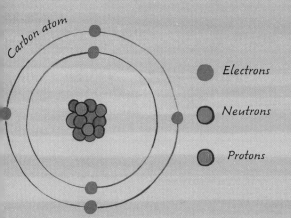

Carbon atom

Electrons

Neutrons

Protons

Atomic structure

The atoms of each element have a set number of protons and electrons. The periodic table puts elements in order of this atomic number, beginning with hydrogen, whose atoms each have one proton and one electron. Carbon has six protons and electrons, so it is sixth on the periodic table.

CARL VON LINDE

German scientist and engineer
1842–1934

Carl's refrigeration machines kick-started a new industry. People quickly found new ways to use them, such as for the very first human-made ice rink, in 1896.

It's hard to imagine life without fridges and freezers. They can be found in many homes around the world.

For thousands of years, people have extracted (taken out) all kinds of interesting things from rocks and soil. Carl von Linde was one of the first people to work out how to extract useful substances from air! As a schoolboy, he visited a cotton mill and was captivated by the machinery. He decided to study mechanical engineering, but lost his place at college after taking part in a student protest.

Carl's teachers helped him get an apprenticeship instead. After working for companies that made steam engines, Carl began teaching engineering at universities. He set up a machine lab for his students, which he also used for his own research.

Separating oxygen from air meant it could be put in tanks and transported anywhere in the world.

The chemical formula for oxygen is O_2.

Refrigeration innovation

Carl was especially curious about how machines might be used to cool things down. In the late 1800s, most factories, homes, and shops still relied on blocks of ice cut from frozen rivers and lakes to keep things cold. Carl set out to improve existing cooling systems, and ended up inventing some of the world's most effective refrigeration machines.

He gave up his teaching job and set up a company to build them for all types of customer — from food makers and dairies, to factories and science labs. However, Carl didn't stop there. He then discovered how to use cooling systems to separate out the different gases in air — mainly oxygen — in quantities big enough to sell. Each gas has different uses when separated from the others. This breakthrough changed the world, because oyxgen could now be stored in tanks and used when needed, such as for patients in hospitals.

Pure oxygen has many uses. It can be found in hospitals around the world, and is even used to burn fuel in space rockets!

OXYGEN

Liquefying air

By squeezing air then letting it expand, over and over again, Carl was able to cool it down enough so it became liquid. Each of the gases in air changes back from a liquid to a gas at a different temperature. By warming the liquid air very slowly, Carl was able to separate out the gases, including oxygen, one by one and put them into tanks. He made machines that could do this with huge amounts of air.

At first, pure oxygen was used in powerful oxyacetylene torches. These burn with a flame so hot that they can melt and cut through metal.

The flame comes out of this end.

These torches made it easier to build skyscrapers, ships, and other steel structures.

ROBERT KOCH
German microbiologist
1843–1910

Staining bacteria

Robert invented new ways to study the tiniest living things. He let bacteria multiply in Petri dishes and stained them to show up better under a microscope. He realized that two species of bacteria can be as different as lions and starfish!

As a doctor in the 1800s, Robert Koch saw patient after patient battling deadly infections, such as tuberculosis, cholera, and diphtheria. Scientists had found clues that infectious diseases were caused by tiny, harmful microbes, or germs, but no one knew why there were so many different types of illness, seemingly caused by the same thing. Robert decided to try to solve the puzzle himself.

He began by looking at a disease called anthrax, which affected many farm animals in Germany at the time. Robert spotted the same, rod-shaped germs in the blood of different animals infected with the disease.

Anthrax bacteria

Robert studied microbes using simple equipment at home.

A huge, tiny discovery

Robert realised that this single type of bacteria could be causing anthrax. It was the first time anyone had worked out that a specific type of bacteria caused a certain disease. People could now try to find the bacteria behind other diseases. This would allow them to work out how to treat, or even prevent, the diseases.

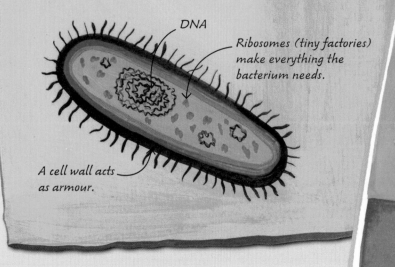

Tuberculosis

In the 1800s, the deadly lung infection tuberculosis (known as TB) was killing a huge number of people each year — and nobody knew what caused it. Robert discovered that the germ responsible was this bacillus (rod-shaped bacterium), shown here at thousands of times its actual size.

DNA

Ribosomes (tiny factories) make everything the bacterium needs.

A cell wall acts as armour.

The founder of bacteriology

Robert travelled the world, identifying the bacteria responsible for dozens of diseases, including the biggest killers at the time — tuberculosis and cholera. He passed on his important knowledge, teaching other scientists how to tell bacteria apart. He also helped authorities make plans for preventing infections and controlling large outbreaks, called epidemics.

Once people knew diseases were caused by microbes, they understood how hygiene measures, such as washing your hands and food, could save many lives. Robert was awarded the Nobel Prize in Medicine, in 1905.

Cholera bacteria

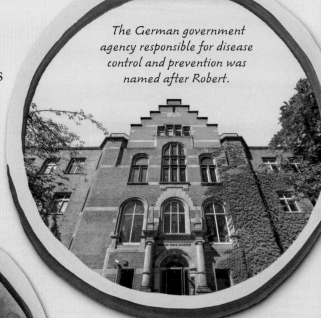

The German government agency responsible for disease control and prevention was named after Robert.

KITASATO SHIBASABURŌ
Japanese doctor and bacteriologist
1853–1931

Kitasato developed the diphtheria antitoxin using blood from horses that were immune to the disease – which means their bodies could fight it off.

As a young scientist, Kitasato Shibasaburō travelled to Berlin, in Germany, to study science. He worked with the famous microbiologist Robert Koch. He examined the bacteria that caused tetanus and diphtheria, and discovered that it wasn't the microbes themselves that caused the symptoms, but the toxins they released.

With his newfound knowledge, Kitasato was able to develop antitoxins to fight the toxins and treat the illnesses. He returned to his home country of Japan in 1892, to put his learning into practice.

In 1894, the Japanese government sent Kitasato to Hong Kong to investigate an outbreak of bubonic plague. He took six assistants and a portable laboratory with him, ready to examine plague victims and solve the mystery of what caused this deadly disease. But three days later, a rival bacteriologist arrived!

Alexandre was the first to link bubonic plague to rats.

ALEXANDRE YERSIN

Swiss-born French doctor, bacteriologist, and explorer • 1863–1943

Alexandre Yersin trained in the laboratory of another great bacteriologist, Louis Pasteur. One of Alexandre's first projects was helping to develop a treatment for a disease called rabies. He later used this discovery to save his own life!

In 1890, Alexandre went to work as a doctor in South East Asia. He built up such a good reputation that in 1894, the French government asked him to visit nearby Hong Kong, to help work out what was causing the bubonic plague.

Bubonic plague

This nasty disease became known as the "Black Death", after it killed around half of all Europeans in just seven years in the 14th century. Thanks to modern medicine, it is no longer common or fatal.

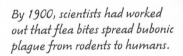

By 1900, scientists had worked out that flea bites spread bubonic plague from rodents to humans.

Both scientists managed to pinpoint and grow the bacteria that caused the plague. Although Kitasato is thought to have found it first, Alexandre found out more about it. Back in Paris, Alexandre made a medicine called an antiserum, which he used to begin treating patients in Hong Kong, in 1896. In the 1970s, the bacteria were renamed *Yersinia pestis* in Alexandre's honour.

Hong Kong was a busy port in the 1890s. Stowed away on the ships, rats brought bubonic plague from Europe.

53

MARIE CURIE

Polish–French physicist and chemist
1867–1934

Marie Curie (born Marie Skłodowska) passed all her secondary school exams a year early. However, she was frustrated to find that Polish universities did not admit girls. Nothing could stand in the way of her passion for science, so Marie worked as a teacher until she raised enough money to move to Paris, in France. There, she could study physics and maths at a top university, the Sorbonne.

A French scientist called Henri Becquerel had recently noticed that the element uranium gave out strange, invisible rays. Marie was curious and began her own research. She was astonished to find that pitchblende — a rock containing a little uranium — gave out much stronger rays than uranium itself! This was a clue that it contained another mysterious substance. Working with her husband, Pierre Curie, Marie set out to investigate.

> Be less curious about people and more curious about ideas.

Breakthrough

After years of grinding down pitchblende and working with the powder, Marie and Pierre extracted two new elements. They named them polonium (after Poland) and radium. The elements gave out so much radiation energy that they glowed in the dark! Marie came up with the word "radioactive" to describe the way they released radiation.

Radioactive rays

Over the next few years, other scientists found dozens of ways to use the intense radiation energy released by radium — from destroying germs in hospitals to getting rid of cancer, a serious illness, in patients. Marie, Pierre, and Henri won a Nobel Prize for Physics and became superstars. They could have made a fortune by selling their knowledge, but instead they decided to share it, to help other scientists with their work.

When Pierre was killed in a road accident, Marie was heartbroken, but she was determined to carry on their quest to understand radioactivity and how it could be used to help people. She became the first person ever to win a second Nobel Prize — this time, for chemistry. Her laboratory in Paris became one of the best places in the world to study radioactivity, and it helped many other women to become scientists. They included Marie's daughter Irene, who went on to win a Nobel Prize of her own!

Radiation can be harmful to those who work with it. Marie's work often made her very ill, and she died of cancer. Today, a charity named after her helps cancer patients. Its symbol is a daffodil.

During World War 1, Marie raised money to set up the first mobile X-ray trucks. They could be driven to where they were most needed, helping to save lives.

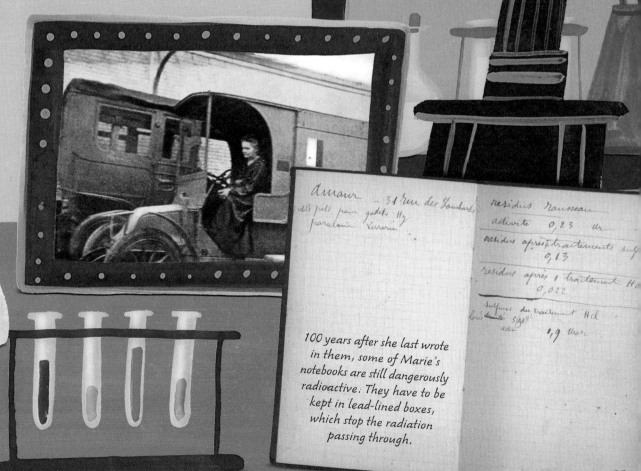

100 years after she last wrote in them, some of Marie's notebooks are still dangerously radioactive. They have to be kept in lead-lined boxes, which stop the radiation passing through.

55

As an army doctor during World War I, Alexander Fleming saw just how deadly simple infections could be. Army hospitals treated far more soldiers for disease than for injuries caused by fighting. After the war, Alexander began hunting for something that could fight the microbes that caused these nasty infections.

At first, he focused on antiseptics, which can kill bacteria or stop them growing. These chemicals can also harm human cells though, so they couldn't be used inside the body. Next, Alexander investigated natural substances with antibacterial effects — including his own snot! Then one day, he stumbled upon a type of mould (fungus) that could stop bacteria in their tracks once and for all.

Bacteria breakthrough

Alexander decided to grow staphylococcus bacteria in Petri dishes. One day in 1928, he noticed mould growing on an unwashed Petri dish. As he went to clean it, he noticed that the bacteria closest to the mould were dying. Could the *mould* be killing them?

Blue-green penicillin mould

Bacteria near the mould has been killed.

Bacteria further away is still alive.

Moulds make bacteria-killing chemicals to defend themselves.

ALEXANDER FLEMING

Scottish doctor and microbiologist • 1881–1955

56

Disease destroyer

The mould was from the penicillium family, so Alexander chose the name "penicillin" for the bacteria-killing chemical it produced. Penicillin destroyed many types of bacteria, including the ones that caused deadly diseases, such as pneumonia, syphilis, and diphtheria. Even better, it didn't harm human cells, unlike antiseptics.

During World War II, other scientists raced to turn penicillin into a medicine that could be given to humans. Howard Florey and Ernst Chain succeeded, and in 1945, they shared the Nobel Prize with Alexander, for the discovery of the world's first "antibiotic". Meanwhile, another scientist called Dorothy Hodgkin was trying to work out the chemical structure of penicillin, so that even better medicines could be made.

After World War II, scientists found more natural antibiotics. These have saved millions of lives around the world, and are still the main weapon we have against harmful bacteria. Some bacteria have become resistant to antibiotics, so there is an ongoing effort to develop new ones.

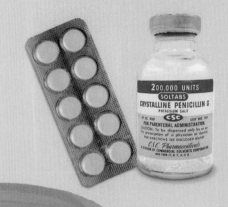

I did not invent penicillin. Nature did that. I only discovered it by accident.

Blue-green penicillium moulds can grow on food when it goes off. We shouldn't eat mouldy foods as many types of mould could be present – including those that can be harmful to humans.

57

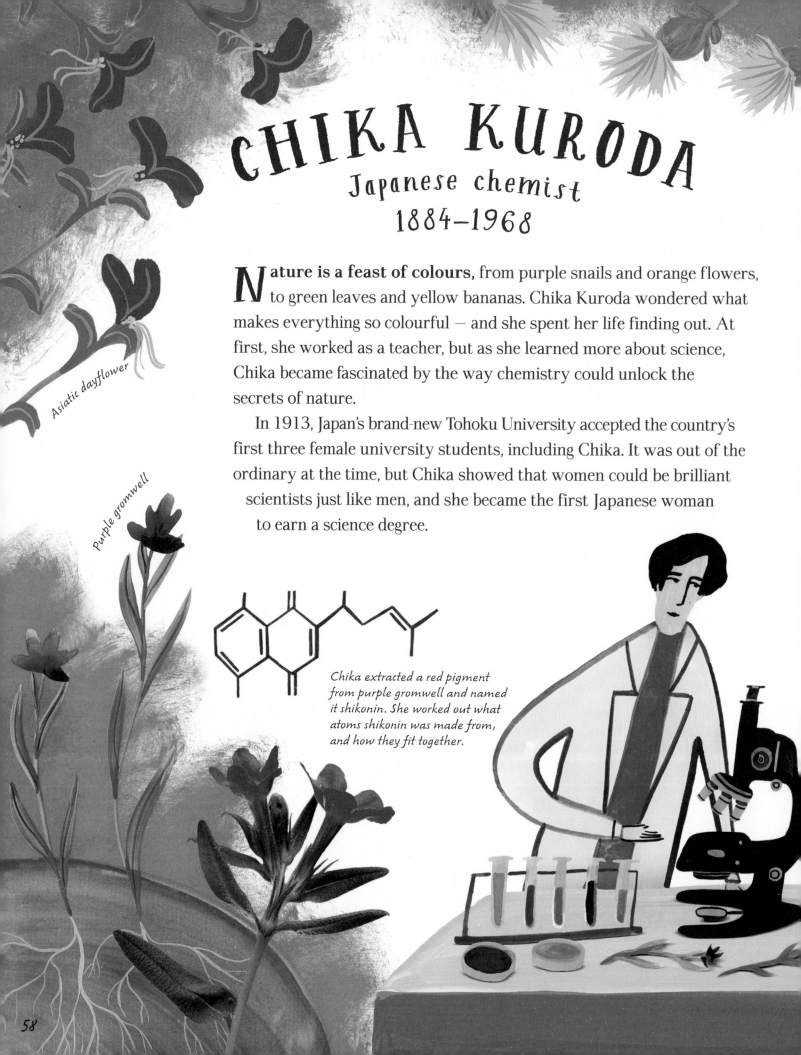

CHIKA KURODA
Japanese chemist
1884–1968

Asiatic dayflower

Purple gromwell

Nature is a feast of colours, from purple snails and orange flowers, to green leaves and yellow bananas. Chika Kuroda wondered what makes everything so colourful — and she spent her life finding out. At first, she worked as a teacher, but as she learned more about science, Chika became fascinated by the way chemistry could unlock the secrets of nature.

In 1913, Japan's brand-new Tohoku University accepted the country's first three female university students, including Chika. It was out of the ordinary at the time, but Chika showed that women could be brilliant scientists just like men, and she became the first Japanese woman to earn a science degree.

Chika extracted a red pigment from purple gromwell and named it shikonin. She worked out what atoms shikonin was made from, and how they fit together.

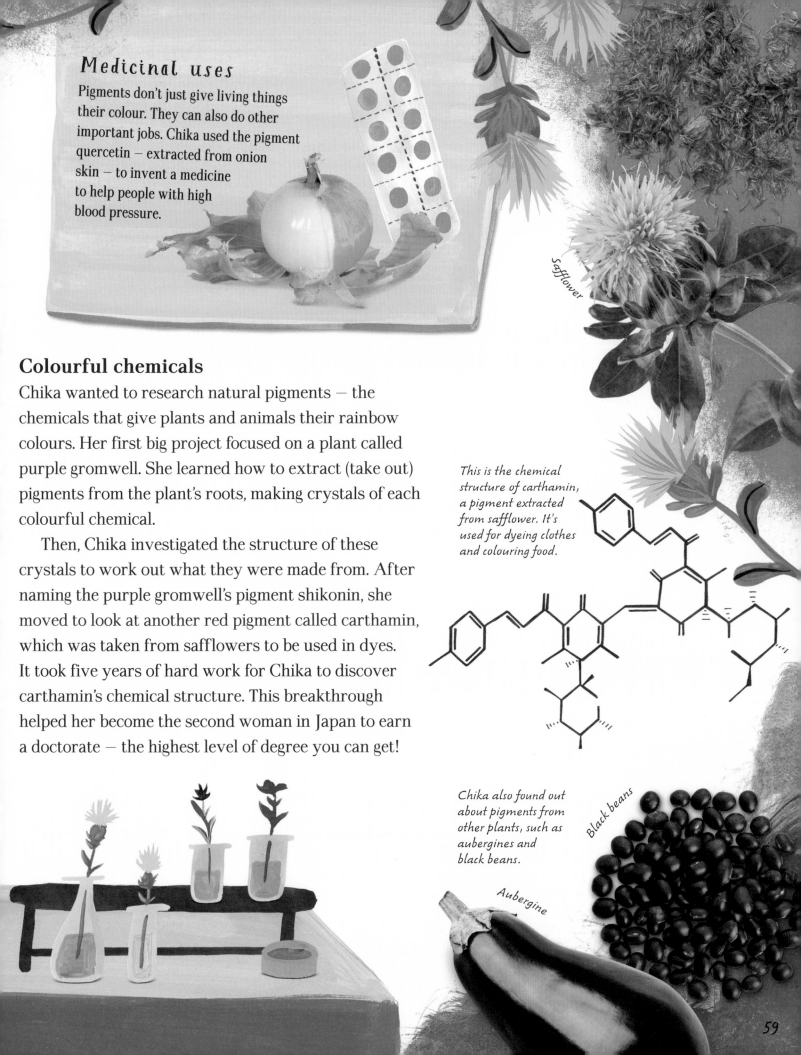

Medicinal uses

Pigments don't just give living things their colour. They can also do other important jobs. Chika used the pigment quercetin – extracted from onion skin – to invent a medicine to help people with high blood pressure.

Safflower

Colourful chemicals

Chika wanted to research natural pigments – the chemicals that give plants and animals their rainbow colours. Her first big project focused on a plant called purple gromwell. She learned how to extract (take out) pigments from the plant's roots, making crystals of each colourful chemical.

Then, Chika investigated the structure of these crystals to work out what they were made from. After naming the purple gromwell's pigment shikonin, she moved to look at another red pigment called carthamin, which was taken from safflowers to be used in dyes. It took five years of hard work for Chika to discover carthamin's chemical structure. This breakthrough helped her become the second woman in Japan to earn a doctorate – the highest level of degree you can get!

This is the chemical structure of carthamin, a pigment extracted from safflower. It's used for dyeing clothes and colouring food.

Chika also found out about pigments from other plants, such as aubergines and black beans.

Black beans

Aubergine

ALICE BALL
American chemist
1892–1916

Alice began her career investigating the chemistry of kava, a plant with a long history in traditional medicine.

Although **Alice Ball** died young, she was able to improve life for thousands of other people. Alice spent part of her childhood in the island state of Hawaii, USA, and decided to return there to study science. In 1915, she became the first woman — and the first African-American — to receive a master's degree in Hawaii.

Alice was brilliant at unlocking the chemistry of plants — working out which substances made certain plants useful as medicines. A local doctor came to her with a problem. Chaulmoogra oil, from the fruits of local trees, was the only treatment he had for a devastating skin illness called Hansen's disease, or leprosy. However, injecting the oil into a patient's bloodstream was painful, because oils and water don't mix, and blood is mainly water. It caused some nasty side-effects in his patients.

Alice's breakthrough made life better for thousands of people.

Hansen's disease

Hansen's disease is caused by a certain type of bacteria, called Mycobacterium leprae. This disease is also known as leprosy. If it is not treated, leprosy can cause painful sores, damage the eyes, and reduce mobility. Today, around 200,000 new cases of leprosy occur each year.

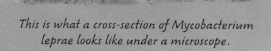

This is what a cross-section of Mycobacterium leprae looks like under a microscope.

Chaulmoogra trees grow in Hawaii and other places with tropical climates. It has velvety fruits, which are filled with oily seeds.

In 1916, Alice became very ill and died. She may have breathed in chlorine gas by mistake while teaching.

The Ball Method

Alice threw herself into solving the problem. In less than a year, she managed to create a different form of the oil. This contained the same bacteria-fighting ingredients as the first version, but the difference was that it could dissolve in water. This made injections much safer and far less painful.

This treatment was introduced in 1916 and used for decades, until a new cure was invented in 1943. Sadly, Alice died before she could see how her work improved life for people suffering from leprosy.

Someone else continued Alice's work with chaulmoogra oil, and even took credit for it. The truth was discovered years later, and the treatment became known as the "Ball Method".

LAB TOOLS

Science begins with observation, and for this, we rely on our senses — sight, hearing, smell, touch, and even taste. Over hundreds of years, scientists have designed a range of tools and instruments to help them control, explore, and measure the world beyond these senses. In turn, these tools and instruments have shaped science itself.

Bunsen burner

These heating devices are a useful tool for science students, as well as in laboratories. They allow gas to be mixed with air before it is burned, which results in a really hot flame — up to 1,500°C (2,732°F)! They were named after Robert Bunsen, who made the first burners based on other people's designs.

Heatproof glass

Glass containers were first used more than 2,000 years ago. Glass doesn't often react to strong chemicals and it is transparent, so you can see experiments as they happen. Today, these containers are usually made with boron oxide, and are called borosilicate glass. This added substance helps glass cope with high temperatures without cracking.

The first pipettes were made from glass tubes with rubber bulbs, but today they are often formed from a single piece of plastic.

Pasteur pipette

Louis Pasteur invented these droppers to move tiny amounts of liquids and microscopic germs from place to place, without mixing them with other things. Squeezing the bulb at the end forces air or liquid out, while releasing it sucks air or liquid up into the tube.

Plastic pipette

Thermometer

This lab tool was created to compare all types of temperature changes more accurately, and there are different temperature scales, such as Celsius, Fahrenheit, and Kelvin. The first thermometers were filled with liquids that take up more space and therefore rise up the thermometer as they get warmer, such as mercury (a type of metal).

Litmus paper

This is no ordinary piece of paper – it contains a mixture of chemicals extracted from lichen. The mixture turns red in acidic liquids, such as lemon juice, and blue in alkaline liquids, such as soap. This makes it quick and easy to find out if a chemical or mixture is acidic or alkaline!

Microscope

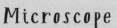

Microscopes let scientists see details that are invisible to our eyes. They have helped us understand what things are made of. The first microscopes bent light to create a bigger picture. Today's most powerful microscopes use beams of electrons instead.

Robert Hooke was one of the first people to make microscopes with more than one or two lenses, which let him see cells for the first time.

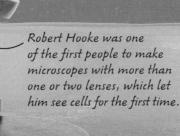

Petri dish

These wide, flat dishes were invented by Julius Petri and are used to grow cultures (large groups) of tiny living things, such as cells. The cover makes sure a culture isn't contaminated by other things, and the dishes slide neatly underneath a microscope lens.

RITA LEVI-MONTALCINI

Rita Levi-Montalcini's training as a doctor left her full of wonder about the beauty and strangeness of life. The question that puzzled her most of all was how a single cell, the size of a speck of dust, grows into a complex animal made up of billions of different cells!

At university, Rita learned how a cell can divide to form two new cells, that go on to divide themselves, in a process called mitosis. However, no one could tell her how these cells became different from one another, each doing different jobs. How did a cell *know* it was supposed to be a nerve cell, for example, rather than a blood cell or a skin cell? It became Rita's mission to find out. She began by studying collections of cells, or tissues, from tiny, unhatched chicken embryos, still growing in their eggs.

The chicken and the egg

Rita studied chicken embryos as they grew from a single, tiny cell into a baby chick. She tried to work out what caused certain cells to develop into nerve cells.

Rita noticed that if she removed certain tissues from a chicken embryo, the nerves didn't grow in the normal way.

Rita's first experiments were all done in her bedroom, while she and her family were in hiding from German forces during World War II.

A powerful protein

After lots of experiments, one thing became clear: the chicken embryo tissues contained some kind of instructions that told new nerve cells to grow. This was different from the theories of other scientists at the time, including Rita's former teacher!

After World War II was over, Rita was invited to repeat her experiments in a professional laboratory, where her exceptional discovery was confirmed. Rita worked with a biochemist called Stanley Cohen to find out more. They discovered a protein (an organic building block) that controls the growth and development of new nerve cells. Rita and Stanley won a Nobel Prize for discovering this "nerve growth factor". Their work has helped scientists and doctors to better understand how cells and organs grow, and what causes certain diseases, such as cancers.

Rita and Stanley worked at Washington University in St Louis, USA.

DOROTHY HODGKIN

British chemist
1910–1994

Dorothy Hodgkin couldn't wait until she was grown up to become a scientist. She turned the attic of her house into a lab, collecting objects she found in nature and analysing them with her chemistry set. However, what captured Dorothy's attention most were the beautiful crystals that formed when certain salts were dissolved in water. She decided to study chemistry at university, so she could keep exploring.

Dorothy learned a new way to unlock the secrets of chemicals. X-rays could be used to peer deep inside the crystal of a chemical, to work out what it was made from. Dorothy focused on chemicals that were important to human health.

To get hold of crystals to examine, Dorothy used a version of the simple experiments she did at school.

1) Dissolve lots of copper sulphate in water.

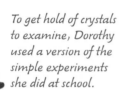

2) The water slowly evaporates (turns to gas).

3) What's left behind is pure copper sulphate. Its molecules have a regular shape, so they pack together neatly to form crystals.

Dorothy's first big discovery was the structure of the antibiotic penicillin. Scientists could now make their own versions of this important medicine.

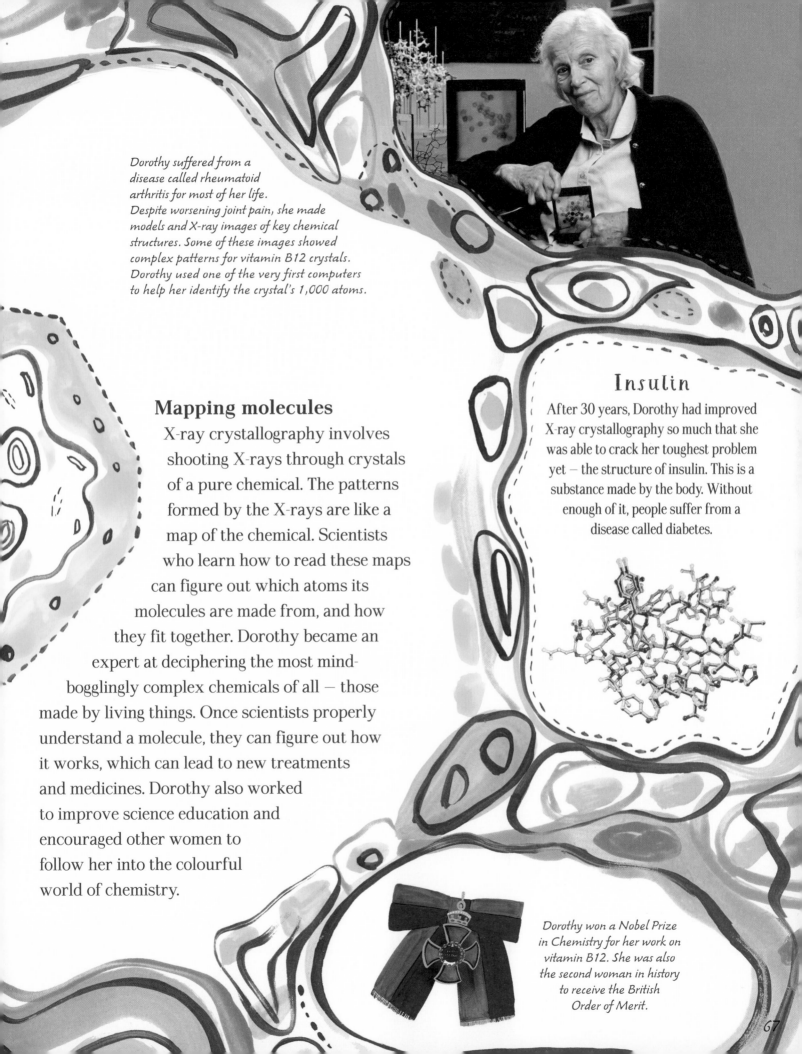

Dorothy suffered from a disease called rheumatoid arthritis for most of her life. Despite worsening joint pain, she made models and X-ray images of key chemical structures. Some of these images showed complex patterns for vitamin B12 crystals. Dorothy used one of the very first computers to help her identify the crystal's 1,000 atoms.

Mapping molecules

X-ray crystallography involves shooting X-rays through crystals of a pure chemical. The patterns formed by the X-rays are like a map of the chemical. Scientists who learn how to read these maps can figure out which atoms its molecules are made from, and how they fit together. Dorothy became an expert at deciphering the most mind-bogglingly complex chemicals of all — those made by living things. Once scientists properly understand a molecule, they can figure out how it works, which can lead to new treatments and medicines. Dorothy also worked to improve science education and encouraged other women to follow her into the colourful world of chemistry.

Insulin

After 30 years, Dorothy had improved X-ray crystallography so much that she was able to crack her toughest problem yet — the structure of insulin. This is a substance made by the body. Without enough of it, people suffer from a disease called diabetes.

Dorothy won a Nobel Prize in Chemistry for her work on vitamin B12. She was also the second woman in history to receive the British Order of Merit.

AKIRA YOSHINO
Japanese chemist
1948–present

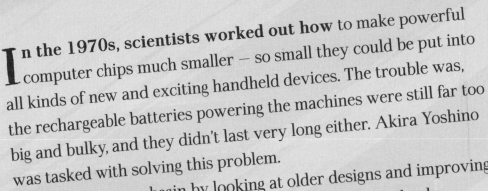

In the 1970s, scientists worked out how to make powerful computer chips much smaller — so small they could be put into all kinds of new and exciting handheld devices. The trouble was, the rechargeable batteries powering the machines were still far too big and bulky, and they didn't last very long either. Akira Yoshino was tasked with solving this problem.

Most inventors begin by looking at older designs and improving them. However, Akira decided to try something completely different. He helped to create the modern lithium-ion battery, which was smaller, lighter, and easier to recharge than the competition.

Martian motor

Electric cars are becoming more popular as people try to use less fossil fuel. By 2040, it is predicted that more than 50 million electric vehicles will be zooming around the world's roads — with a handful on other planets too!

Opportunity was an electric vehicle that drove around Mars for more than 10 years.

Rechargeable batteries will be an important part of a fossil fuel-free future, because they can store electricity from renewable sources.

Electrifying the future

Akira discovered that using carbon in a lithium-ion battery made it safer than earlier versions. He applied for a patent for his battery in 1985. A patent is a special document that describes what is new about an invention and gives the owner the right to be the only one to sell it for a certain time. The first lithium-ion batteries were sold in 1991 – around 10 years after development began!

Lithium-ion batteries have continued to get thinner and lighter. They are now found in laptops, phones, tablets, and games consoles. Larger versions have been key in developing electric vehicles. Today, almost 65 per cent of the lithium produced each year is used to make batteries. There are still technological and environmental problems to solve, but Akira's work on this rechargable energy source has paved the way towards a future free from fossil fuels, such as oil.

In 2019, Akira shared the Nobel Prize in Chemistry for his work.

QUARRAISHA ABDOOL KARIM

Indian-origin South African epidemiologist • 1960-present

Quarraisha tries to understand how and why diseases spread in communities. This area of science is called epidemiology.

Science appealed to Quarraisha because it gave her a way to help people. As a young researcher, she began studying a virus that was affecting more and more people in South Africa and around the world – human immunodeficiency virus (HIV). This virus damages cells in the body's immune system, which fights off diseases. Over time, a patient's immune system can become so weak that they can no longer get rid of everyday infections, such as flu. People with HIV are also much more likely to get certain types of cancer. This condition is called acquired immunodeficiency syndrome (AIDS).

This is what HIV looks like under a powerful microscope.

Understanding the virus

Doctors already knew that the HIV virus is passed from person to person in certain body fluids, such as blood. However, some groups of people were more likely to become infected by it than others.

In the early 1990s, Quarraisha discovered that in South Africa, young people — and especially teenage girls — were most at risk. She decided to devote her career to understanding why, and to using her discoveries to find new ways to prevent the virus from spreading.

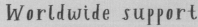

Worldwide support

A red ribbon is a symbol of awareness (knowledge of) and support for people living with HIV around the world. Quarraisha leads a large team of researchers, who try to find vaccines, treatments, and cures for HIV and AIDS.

By working closely with communities in South Africa, Quarraisha discovered that young women couldn't easily find information about health. They didn't like asking adults for advice, and preferred to talk about it with their friends. She worked out that without expert knowledge, false information could spread quickly.

Quarraisha suggested that girls and young women should be taught how to avoid catching the virus. She also developed a medicine that stops the virus spreading, especially among women. Nearly 8 million South Africans suffer from HIV, but Quarraisha's work has already provided treatment to many of them.

FANTASTIC
PHYSICS

How can we explain the Universe? Physicists' ultimate goal is to find one answer that can explain everything — the movements of stars and galaxies, the behaviour of particles smaller than atoms, the different forms of energy, and the mysterious, undetectable dark matter.

In the 1500s and 1600s, many beliefs about how the world worked were based on old ideas from ancient Greece. They included concepts that seem very strange to us now — such as the belief that the Earth was at the centre of the Universe — orbited by the Sun, planets, and stars!

Galileo Galilei was a very creative person. He was not afraid to question these old ideas and come up with new ones. To do this, Galileo observed things carefully, building his own instruments, such as telescopes, to get a better look. He designed experiments to test ideas and find out what was really happening. The things he discovered may seem obvious to us now, but many people at the time disagreed with him.

Centre of the Solar System

A Polish astronomer called Nicolaus Copernicus had the idea that the Earth was travelling around the Sun. By studying the night sky with a telescope, Galileo found evidence that proved Nicolaus was right. This upset many powerful people, and Galileo was ordered to stay at home and stop spreading the truth. But nothing could stop him from working.

Before Galileo, most people wrongly believed that the Sun orbited the Earth, not the other way around.

Galileo didn't invent telescopes, but he improved them by making his own lenses — the curved pieces of glass inside that make objects look bigger.

GALILEO GALILEI
Italian mathematician and astronomer
1564–1642

A man of many talents

Galileo was a polymath, which means that he was good at lots of things! He wrote poetry, played music, painted pictures, and studied medicine. Mathematics was his favourite subject though, and he used it to solve real world problems. For example, he worked out that things didn't stop moving because they ran out of pushing force, but because friction slowed them down. Isaac Newton based his first two laws of motion on Galileo's discoveries. We still use these laws today to understand how all kinds of objects move.

Galileo used a telescope to observe the Moon. He drew maps of the craters on its surface.

Experiments helped Galileo to find out why objects move as they do. For example, he proved that when objects are flung through the air, they travel in a smooth, curved shape, called a parabola.

Galileo rolled metal balls down ramps to measure how objects speed up as they fall.

It is a beautiful and delightful sight to behold the body of the Moon.

There were no reliable clocks in Galileo's day, so he often used his own pulse to measure time. He described how a clock might use a swinging pendulum to keep time, but he died before his idea was proved right.

75

Gravity

Isaac thought of gravity as a force that pulls objects towards each other. He explained that every object has gravitational force, but the more massive an object, the stronger the pull.

Gravity pulls planets into orbit around the Sun.

Isaac was said to have come up with his theory of gravity while watching an apple fall from a tree, but this is probably a myth!

As a teenager, Isaac Newton was put in charge of his family's farm. However, his mind was on other things. He loved figuring out how mechanical objects worked, and how to build his own. His projects included a clock powered by water and a model windmill powered by a mouse! Finally, his mother decided he would be better suited to studying at university than running a farm.

Isaac was so focused on his work that he didn't spend much time with other people, and was often distracted when they spoke to him. Unfortunately, a disease called the Great Plague spread across Europe a few years into his study. The university shut, and Isaac got to work studying by himself.

Isaac's most famous book, the Principia, has 500 pages of brilliant ideas.

ISAAC NEWTON
English physicist • 1642–1727

A force for change

Isaac began to come up with many amazing ideas. He invented calculus, which is a mathematical method of working things out. He explored light, suggesting that it was made up of many colours. Isaac's most well-known discovery was gravity. This is the force that keeps us on the Earth, and our planet circling the Sun.

Isaac continued to study the invisible forces of the world. He wrote three "laws of motion" to explain why objects move as they do.

Rainbow of colours

To learn about light, Isaac passed beams of it through a glass prism. He discovered that light came out of the prism as different colours. Isaac used his findings to work out that light is a mixture of colours.

As well as ideas, Isaac came up with inventions, such as the reflecting telescope.

Isaac's pet dog, Diamond, once knocked over a candle and set fire to important work!

Isaac's ideas about gravity and motion help explain all sorts of things — from the movement of planets to the speed of sound. Whenever someone kicks a football, drives a car, or launches a rocket, Isaac's laws of motion explain how it will move.

Isaac also changed the way science is done. He carried out experiments to test his ideas, which was unusual at the time. Now, scientists rely on experiments to help prove their ideas.

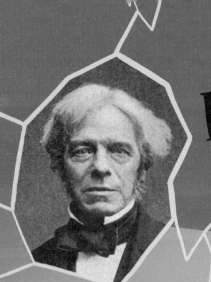

MICHAEL FARADAY
English natural scientist
1791–1867

Michael Faraday was born in London, England, at the beginning of the Industrial Revolution — a time when lots of new machinery was being invented to increase the speed of manufacturing. Like many children at the time, Michael left school aged 13 to begin earning money. For seven years, he learned how to make books, as an apprentice bookbinder. But, it was what was inside the books that would interest Michael the most. He read one book about science and was hooked.

Michael began seeking out science books to teach himself about the subject. At 20, he watched a public talk given by a famous scientist called Humphrey Davy. Michael was fascinated, and decided to write to Humphrey to share his own questions and ideas. A year later, he became Humphrey's assistant.

Making electricity

Using his knowledge about electricity and magnetism, Michael made an electric motor — a machine that converts electrical energy into movement energy. He then invented the dynamo — the first generator, which converted movement into electricity.

Michael used coils of wire to create electromagnets, which are metal objects made magnetic by electricity.

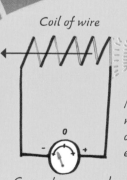

Coil of wire

To and fro movement

Magnet

Current measured

Michael discovered that moving a magnet in and out of a coil of wire caused electricity to flow in the wire.

A bright spark

At first, Michael worked on projects involving combustion (burning) and explosive chemicals.

However, he soon became captivated by a new discovery in physics: when electricity flows through a metal wire, it turns the wire into a weak magnet.

Alongside his work for Humphrey, Michael quietly started his own research. In 1821, he worked out how to arrange a wire and magnet so that when electricity passed through the wire, it began swinging around the magnet in a circle. He had invented the electric motor — changing electricity into movement for the first time in history.

Lighthouses once used oil lamps and reflective surfaces for light. Michael spent years looking for a way to use a generator instead. Finally, in 1858, electric lighting was installed in a working lighthouse for the first time, with Michael's approval.

Electric light first shone out to sea from the South Foreland Lighthouse in Dover, UK.

Michael gave amazing science lectures at the Royal Institution in London, to inspire children just as he had been inspired by Humphrey Davy.

In 1822, Michael scribbled a reminder in his diary to try the experiment in reverse. Ten years later, he finally got around to the task — and showed that it was possible to generate electricity using magnets and movement. Now there was a way to produce electricity without needing to use batteries, which can run out. Michael's ideas and discoveries sparked an age of invention and experimentation!

Michael helped Humphrey Davy invent a lamp that was safe to use in coal mines. Before that, lamps often caused explosions.

ERNEST RUTHERFORD

New Zealand–born British physicist • 1871–1937

Some scientists become famous for one world-changing discovery. Ernest Rutherford made three! The most important was that atoms are mostly empty space. This set the stage for all kinds of new findings about atoms and radiation, a type of energy.

Ernest went on to explain what makes certain things — known as radioactive substances — give off radiation. He also named the proton, one of the three tiny particles that are the building blocks of all atoms.

Having grown up on a farm without easy access to a good scientific education, Ernest worked hard to help other physics students succeed. Many of the students he trained made incredible discoveries themselves. As well as helping individuals, he also changed the world — by beginning the science of nuclear physics.

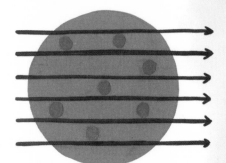

People used to think the matter in an atom was spread out equally, so radiation would pass through in straight lines.

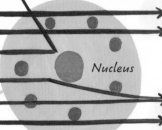

Ernest fired radiation at a foil of gold atoms. Some radiation hit a detector in different places than if it had simply passed straight through the foil.

Nucleus

The way radiation was deflected told Ernest that most of the matter in an atom was clustered at the centre — the nucleus.

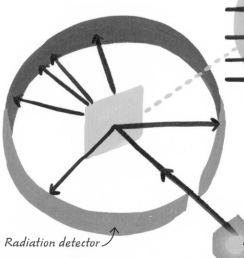

Radiation detector

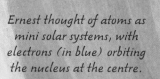

Source of radiation

Ernest thought of atoms as mini solar systems, with electrons (in blue) orbiting the nucleus at the centre.

NIELS BOHR
Danish physicist
1885–1962

Niels improved Ernest's model of how atoms work.

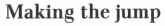

Niels Bohr had a very different childhood to Ernest. His father was a scientist who was nominated for a Nobel Prize – twice! As a young scientist, Niels had the opportunity to work alongside Ernest at the University of Manchester in the UK. He delved deeper into Ernest's idea of the atomic structure. He focused on the electrons – the particles that orbit, or move around, the nucleus at the centre of the atom. Niels taught us to think of electrons orbiting the nucleus in layers.

Making the jump

Experiments showed that Niels's model was great at explaining puzzling things, such as why different atoms glow with different colours when heated. As atoms soak up energy, their electrons can jump up one or more layers. When the electrons return to their original places, the energy they gained is released as light.

Niels's ideas were soon being used to explain and predict characteristics of elements. With better understanding of nuclear energy, people could use it in new ways, for example as a source of power.

Breaking the centre of atoms apart releases huge amounts of energy. Niels predicted that this could be used to make powerful bombs. The world's first nuclear bomb was detonated in 1945, during World War II.

After World War II, Niels worked to find non-violent ways that nuclear physics could be used. He was one of the people that set up CERN in Europe, where scientists from all around the world study atoms and even smaller particles.

81

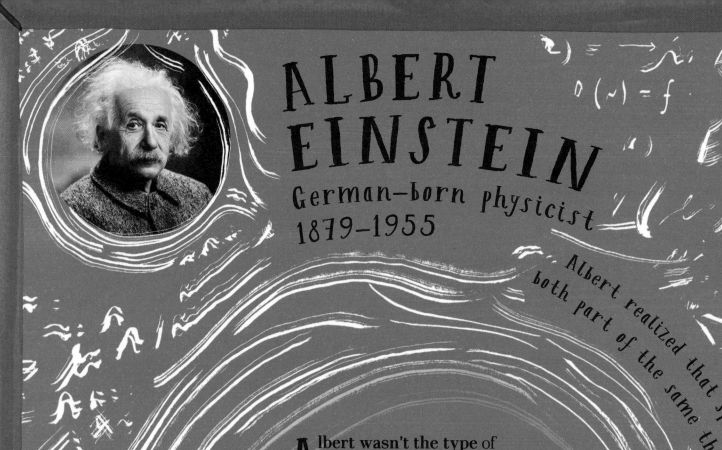

ALBERT EINSTEIN

German-born physicist
1879–1955

Albert realized that space and time are both part of the same thing — space-time.

Albert wasn't the type of physicist that gazes at stars or drops balls off towers to see how they fall. He was a theoretical physicist who explored the Universe in his mind. His "thought experiments" involving light and gravitational force helped him come up with new theories to explain how the Universe works. Albert used maths as a language to describe the Universe, and to test his ideas.

In just one year, Albert published theories that changed the way we understand light, atoms, moving objects, energy, time, and gravity. He became a scientific superstar and more than 100 years later, his last name is still used to mean "genius".

Airy atoms

Albert realized that the specks of dust you see in a beam of sunlight are being pushed around by jiggling atoms of air. This was the first proof that atoms are real.

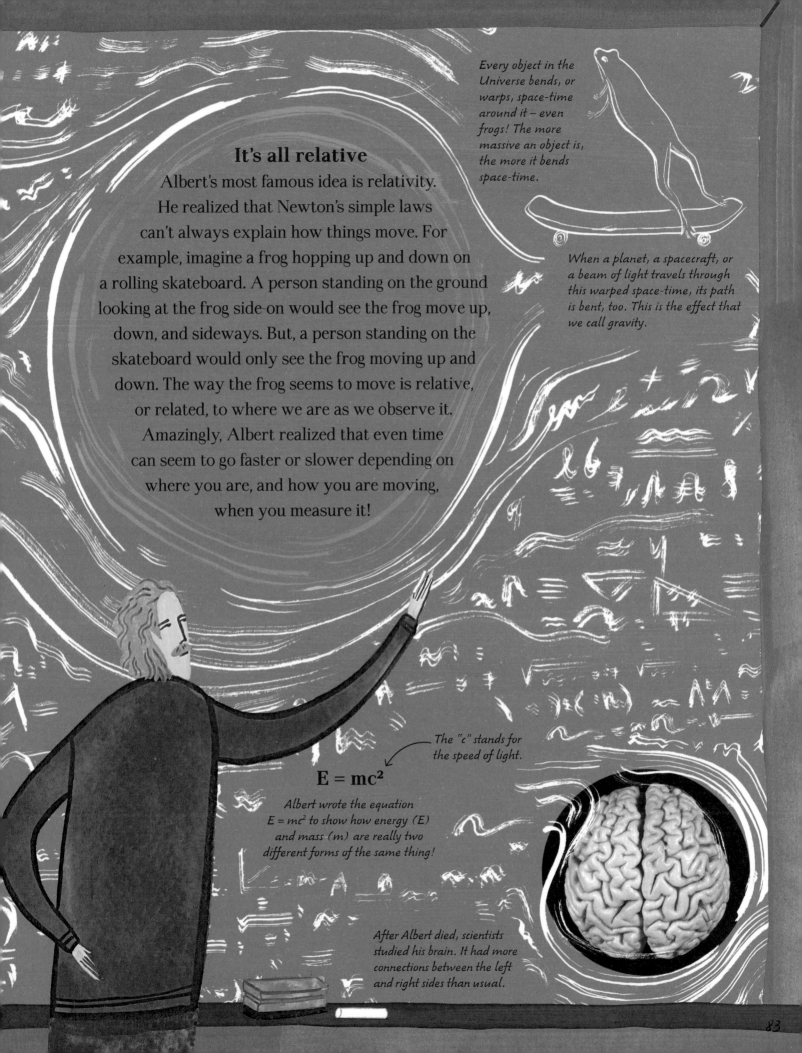

It's all relative

Albert's most famous idea is relativity.
He realized that Newton's simple laws
can't always explain how things move. For
example, imagine a frog hopping up and down on
a rolling skateboard. A person standing on the ground
looking at the frog side-on would see the frog move up,
down, and sideways. But, a person standing on the
skateboard would only see the frog moving up and
down. The way the frog seems to move is relative,
or related, to where we are as we observe it.
Amazingly, Albert realized that even time
can seem to go faster or slower depending on
where you are, and how you are moving,
when you measure it!

*Every object in the
Universe bends, or
warps, space-time
around it – even
frogs! The more
massive an object is,
the more it bends
space-time.*

*When a planet, a spacecraft, or
a beam of light travels through
this warped space-time, its path
is bent, too. This is the effect that
we call gravity.*

*The "c" stands for
the speed of light.*

$$E = mc^2$$

*Albert wrote the equation
$E = mc^2$ to show how energy (E)
and mass (m) are really two
different forms of the same thing!*

*After Albert died, scientists
studied his brain. It had more
connections between the left
and right sides than usual.*

EMMY NOETHER

German mathematician
1882–1935

Noether's theorem explains why the laws of physics stay the same everywhere in the Universe.

Emmy Noether was determined to follow in her father's footsteps and become a mathematician. At the time in Germany, girls weren't allowed to study for a degree at university. They could sit in on classes, though, which is exactly what Emmy did, at the University of Erlangen. She was one of only two women among thousands of male students!

Slowly, the rules changed and by 1907, Emmy had managed to become a student of maths and even earn a doctorate — the highest qualification you can get. The next challenge was to get a job, at a time when most people still thought mathematicians had to be men.

Noether's theorem helps explain how air flows over a plane's wing.

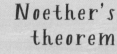

Emmy did her most famous research at the University of Göttingen, Germany.

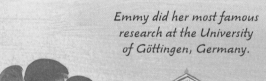

Noether's theorem

When physicists are explaining strange things — such as how birds sit on power lines without getting electric shocks — they make use of Emmy's famous work, known as "Noether's theorem". Emmy used maths, and this theorem, to describe symmetry in the world around us.

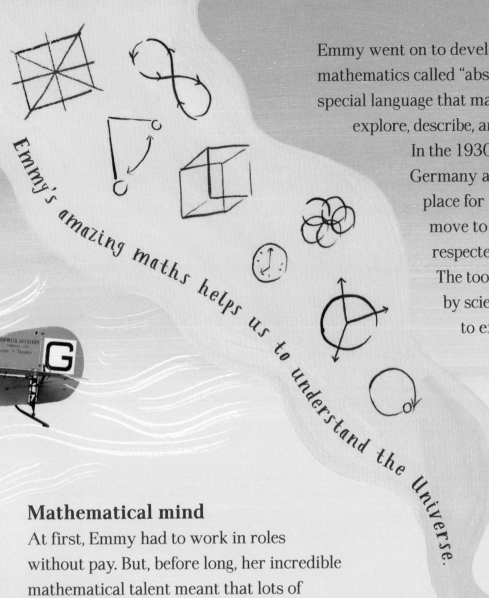

Emmy's amazing maths helps us to understand the Universe.

Emmy went on to develop a whole new type of mathematics called "abstract algebra", which is like a special language that mathematicians and scientists use to explore, describe, and understand the Universe better. In the 1930s, a group called the Nazis ruled Germany and it became a very dangerous place for Jewish people. Emmy decided to move to the USA. She quickly became as respected there as she had been in Europe. The tools she developed have been used by scientists all over the world, helping to explain everything from the behaviour of tiny particles to the gravity of black holes.

Mathematical mind

At first, Emmy had to work in roles without pay. But, before long, her incredible mathematical talent meant that lots of leading scientists and mathematicians wanted to work with her.

Emmy helped to solve a puzzle thrown up by Albert Einstein's new theory of gravity. She proved two mathematical theorems, or rules, that are now woven into all kinds of physics. Many people, including Albert himself, demanded that Emmy be paid for her work. In 1922, she was finally given a role as a university researcher and professor.

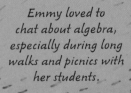

Emmy loved to chat about algebra, especially during long walks and picnics with her students.

ERWIN SCHRÖDINGER
Austrian physicist and philosopher
1887–1961

Science doesn't have to be done indoors. Next to the beautiful Lake Zürich, in Switzerland, Erwin Schrödinger conducted experiments in his mind. In summertime, he even delivered classes in bathing trunks on a beach by the lake! His experiments used maths to describe and predict things that happen in the Universe.

Erwin was particularly interested in working out what goes on inside atoms. He hoped that the behaviour of tiny particles would explain some of the weird and wonderful things in the world. For example, he worked out why substances glow with specific colours of light when they get a boost of light or heat energy.

$$H(t)|\psi(t)\rangle = i\hbar\frac{\partial}{\partial t}|\psi(t)\rangle$$

Erwin's ideas, written in the language of mathematics, were the beginning of a new type of science that focused on how particles behave – quantum mechanics.

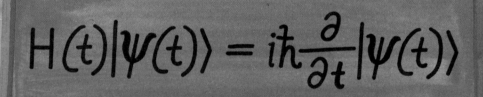

No real cats were used in Erwin's famous thought experiment!

Schrödinger's cat

Erwin's most famous thought experiment imagines that a cat in a closed box will die if a single particle breaks apart. Quantum mechanics doesn't tell us exactly when this will happen — only the probability that it will happen after a certain time. So, the conclusion is that the cat could be both alive and dead at the same time.

The Schrödinger crater is a huge Moon crater, named in Erwin's honour.

Science and politics

In 1933, Erwin was awarded the Nobel Prize in Physics. He moved to Germany and began working alongside Albert Einstein. However, life in Germany was changing quickly. The country was now ruled by the Nazi Party and their leader, Adolf Hitler. The Nazis began by taking away the right of many people, including all Jewish people, to live like everyone else in Germany — they even banned them from certain jobs.

Erwin disagreed with the way the Nazis treated Jewish people and, like many other leading scientists, he decided to leave Germany. Erwin worked in universities around the world, before returning permanently to his home country of Austria in 1955.

In his book What is Life?, Erwin used the word "code" to describe how genes carry information — before DNA was found.

"I do not know whether my way of approach is really the best and simplest. But, in short, it was mine."

Computer scientists, or coders, write the instructions that tell computers what to do. Computers only understand one language, called binary. It's a language that uses just two digits: 0 and 1. This sounds pretty simple, but it's hard for humans to read and write in binary. Grace Hopper created tools that made it possible to give computers instructions using familiar words, rather than 0s and 1s. Her work made it easier for humans to tell computers what to do.

Grace's journey into the exciting world of computer science started with mathematics. She studied maths to the highest possible level, then found a practical way to use her skills by joining the US Navy during World War II. Grace was assigned to the Bureau of Ships Computation Project, at Harvard University.

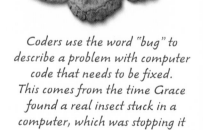

Grace was a very curious child. She once took apart seven different clocks to find out how they worked!

Coders use the word "bug" to describe a problem with computer code that needs to be fixed. This comes from the time Grace found a real insect stuck in a computer, which was stopping it from working properly!

GRACE HOPPER

American computer scientist and US Navy officer • 1906–1992

Harvard Mark I

At Harvard University, Grace began working with with one of the world's very first computers – the Harvard Mark I. It was so huge that it filled an entire room, and it carried out complicated calculations that were needed to design top-secret weapons during the war. Grace learned to program the Mark I by translating numbers and mathematical symbols into binary code.

Brilliant binary

After the war, Grace helped to develop new and better computers, including the first-ever completely electronic computer. She led a team to develop the first computer language compiler, which could quickly carry out the boring job of translating mathematical code into binary.

Next, Grace and her team developed a programming language that used words rather than just numbers and symbols. Again, a compiler did the job of translating the words into binary instructions that the machine could understand. This made it far easier for people who weren't mathematicians to work with computers. The age of computers had begun.

Soon, many different programming languages were being developed. Grace focused on a language called COBOL. She helped to turn it into the most widely used computer language in the world.

Grace loved trying new things. Here, she is coding instructions on punch tape.

The missile destroyer USS Hopper was named after Grace. She was the oldest serving officer in the US Navy when she retired at 79 years old.

Analytical engine

Around 200 years ago, Charles Babbage made plans for a mechanical device that could carry out complicated calculations. This "analytical engine" would have been the first true computer, and it was mechanical, rather than electronic. However, Charles never managed to build it.

In 1991, the Science Museum in London, UK, built this working model of another of Charles's calculating machines, the Difference Engine No 2.

1837

1945

ENIAC

In World War II, ENIAC (Electronic Numerical Integrator and Computer) was designed to carry out calculations for cracking enemy codes. It was the first fully electronic computer, and calculated 1,000 times faster than mechanical computers.

BUILDING COMPUTERS

As well as writing instructions for computers to follow, scientists and engineers also design the parts of a computer that we can touch — known as hardware. The way computers look — and what's inside — is always changing.

1623

This calculating clock replica is found in the Deutsches Museum, in Germany.

Calculators

Way back in the 1620s, this "calculating clock" was designed to carry out boring and complicated calculations so that astronomers didn't have to! They began with a sum, then turned the rods and dials to show the answer.

1971

The Intel 4004 microprocessor was about the size of a fingernail!

Processors

A computer's processor receives and works out information. It then tells output devices what to do, for example, to display the answer to a sum. In the 1970s, much smaller "microprocessors" were invented.

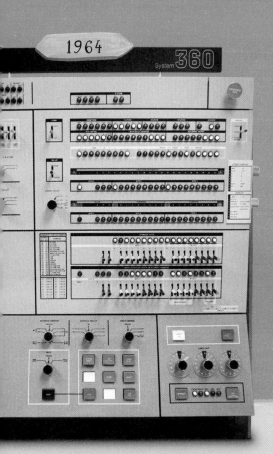

1964

2000

Portable computers

Thanks to new technology and materials, personal computers have become more powerful, easier to use, and smaller. Today, billions of people carry computers in their pockets that can do far more than ENIAC.

Early laptops in the 1980s looked more like desktop computers!

1981

IBM System/360

By the 1960s, electronic computers were affordable enough to be used by all kinds of businesses and labs. Business computers, such as the IBM System/360, could run different sets of instructions, called "programs", so they could be used for lots of different tasks.

Robots

A robot is a machine that works automatically, controlled by a computer. They do different jobs, including dull ones that humans might not want to do! In homes, robotic vacuum cleaners can clean, and in factories, robot arms assemble things.

1996

The first handheld computers went on sale in the 1990s.

IBM Personal Computer

Once microprocessors were available, computers could be made small enough (and cheap enough) for people to have in their homes! This was one of the very first personal computers — or "PCs" for short.

Present

Smartphones are computers and telephones all in one.

1981

MARY GOLDA ROSS
Native American mathematician and engineer • 1908–2008

Mary helped to design P-38 Lightning fighter planes.

Top-secret Skunk Works projects were developed in a tent at the Lockheed base.

Mary's great-great-grandfather was a famous leader of the Cherokee Nation, a large tribe of Native American people in the USA. The Cherokee believed that girls and boys should be educated equally, but that was not the law in the early 1900s in the USA. Mary often found that she was the only girl in her mathematics and science classes, but she didn't mind.

Mary earned a degree in mathematics and worked as a teacher, before joining the engineering company Lockheed in 1942. Her new employer quickly spotted her extraordinary mathematical ability and sent her to university to train as an aeronautical engineer.

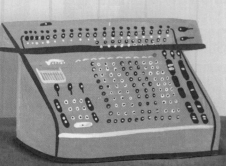

Mary used an early computer for her complex mathematics.

Mary worked on the Gemini-Agena Target Vehicle (GATV). Its most important job was helping spacecraft to dock safely with others in space.

To the stars

Mary was brought into a group of engineering experts at Lockheed, known as Skunk Works. At first, the wonder-team was tasked with designing missiles and defence systems. It was ground-breaking work, and Mary was also making history herself, as both the first Native American aerospace engineer and the only woman in the group of 40 engineers.

The USA then set its sights on space, and Mary used mathematics to help work out how to send a satellite into space for the first time. She did calculations to predict how the spacecraft would behave when moving through the Earth's atmosphere, and how to make sure it stayed on the right path. Later, Mary helped to plan for missions to Mars and Venus. Even now, her work is still classified (top-secret)!

Lifting off

The GATV was carried into space by an Atlas rocket. Once in space, NASA used it to plan and test manoeuvres such as changing orbit. This was important preparation for the Apollo program, which took astronauts to the Moon.

Mary's life work was honoured by a special $1 coin.

CHIEN-SHIUNG WU

Chinese-American nuclear physicist
1912–1997

Chien-Shiung Wu's story shows that shutting people out of science because of their gender or race is not just unfair, but it can also delay amazing discoveries. Chien-Shiung grew up in a small town in China. She moved to the USA to complete her studies in nuclear physics, but at first found it impossible to get a job as a researcher because she was a woman. However, everything changed during World War II. Chien-Shiung began working on the Manhattan Project — a project to build the first nuclear bombs. After the war, she stayed in the USA, becoming a professor of physics at Columbia University. The Manhattan Project taught scientists about radioactivity — when atoms release radioactive energy. Chien-Shiung began studying radioactive atoms that spontaneously (without any help) change into atoms of a different element, releasing tiny, fast-moving electrons in the process. This type of radioactive decay is called beta decay.

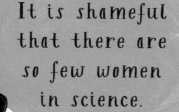

It is shameful that there are so few women in science.

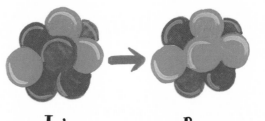

Li → Be → e

Chien-Shiung and her team studied what happened to an atom of lithium (Li) when it decays into an atom of beryllium (Be) — a fast-moving electron (e) is released.

Working together

In the 1950s, Tsung-Dao Lee and Chen Ning Yang asked Chien-Shiung to design an experiment to test their new ideas about beta decay. In 1957, the pair won the Nobel Prize in Physics for their theory — but Chien-Shiung was left out. Afterwards, she began to speak out about the unfair treatment of women in science.

Chen Ning Yang

Tsung-Dao Lee

Changing everything

Chien-Shiung became known for her brilliant experiments. For her Nobel-Prize-winning work with Tsung-Dao Lee and Chen Ning Yang, she cooled radioactive cobalt atoms so much that they stopped jiggling around and lined up neatly in a magnetic field.

Once the atoms were lined up neatly, Chien-Shiung made them spin in different directions, and measured where the electrons from beta decay zoomed out.

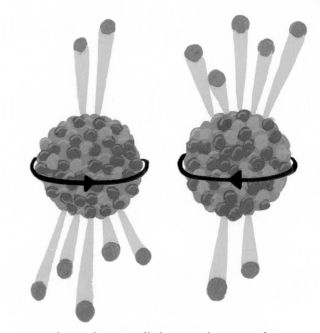

This is what scientists believed would happen before Chien-Shiung's work.

This is what actually happened, proving that some of the forces at the very centre of atoms are not symmetrical (act the same way in every direction), but left-focused.

The "Wu experiment" changed physics forever. It proved that radioactive forces didn't obey the laws of symmetry that everything else in the Universe seemed to follow. This clue helped unlock all sorts of other mysteries, helping us understand how particles can cling together to form things, such as rocks, metals, and even people!

Chien-Shiung won the National Medal of Science and was the first woman to become president of the American Physical Society.

ALBERT BAEZ

Mexican physicist and educator
1912–2007

Albert was born in Mexico, but grew up in New York City, USA. After studying maths and physics, he began research into the uses of X-rays. He was interested in using these invisible rays to make more powerful microscopes.

Normal microscopes collect the light bouncing off an object and pass it through glass lenses. As light passes from air to glass it slows down and changes direction. This bending — known as refraction — causes the object to appear bigger through the glass. Albert wanted to use X-rays instead of light, but X-rays are not refracted by glass.

> Unusual talent in science must be sought out and nurtured because it is more precious than gold or uranium.

Albert worked with a scientist called Paul Kirkpatrick on a design for an X-ray microscope. A strong-enough source of X-rays was found 20 years later, which meant Albert and Paul's system could finally be used.

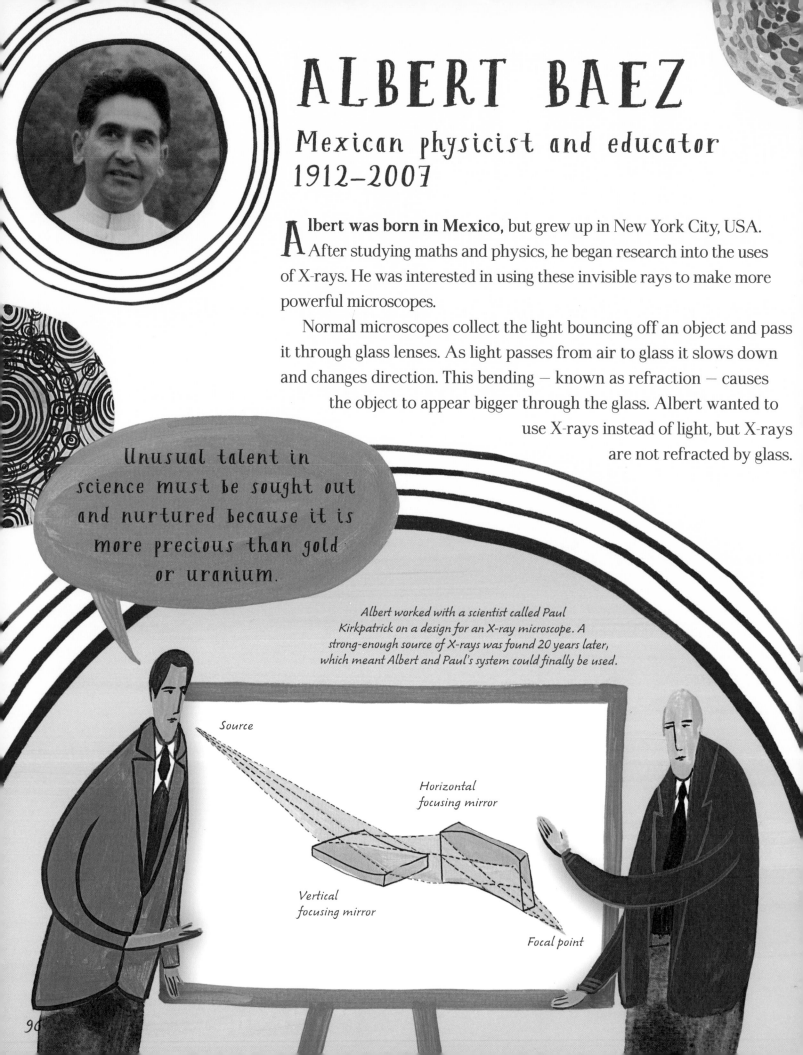

Source

Horizontal focusing mirror

Vertical focusing mirror

Focal point

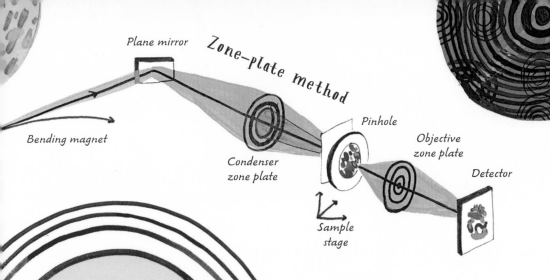

Zone-plate method

Plane mirror

Bending magnet

Condenser zone plate

Pinhole

Sample stage

Objective zone plate

Detector

Today, the zone-plate technology Albert pioneered is used inside the world's highest-resolution X-ray microscopes, allowing us to see...

In the zone

Albert worked on a second method of focusing X-rays, using rings of material called zone-plates. When the rays hit the detector, they form patterns, revealing key information about the particle being studied.

X-ray vision

Albert helped develop a way to focus X-rays on an object by bouncing them off mirrors. It took many years to make these microscopes, but the results were amazing. A beam of X-rays could be focused on a spot 200 times narrower than a human hair! This allowed scientists to see much smaller details than they could with light microscopes. In addition, X-rays can pass through many materials that block visible light. Using these microscopes, scientists could peer inside living cells without needing to destroy them.

Albert believed that the three most important qualities for a scientist were curiosity, creativity, and compassion. He helped spread this message after finishing his research career, working to improve science education around the world.

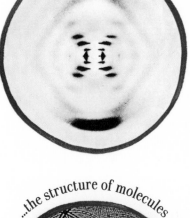

...inside living cells

...the structure of molecules

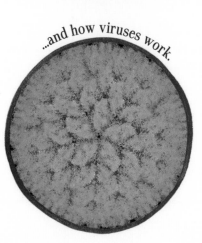

...and how viruses work.

Zone-plate technology is used in telescopes that collect X-rays zooming towards the Earth from objects in space. They give us a better view of distant galaxies, from which very little visible light reaches the Earth.

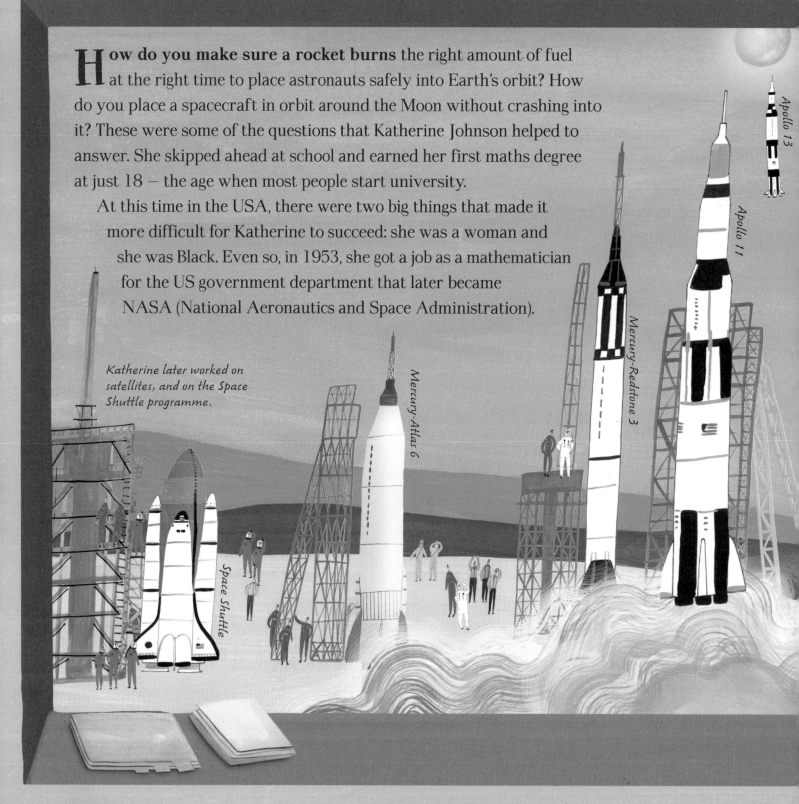

How do you make sure a rocket burns the right amount of fuel at the right time to place astronauts safely into Earth's orbit? How do you place a spacecraft in orbit around the Moon without crashing into it? These were some of the questions that Katherine Johnson helped to answer. She skipped ahead at school and earned her first maths degree at just 18 – the age when most people start university.

At this time in the USA, there were two big things that made it more difficult for Katherine to succeed: she was a woman and she was Black. Even so, in 1953, she got a job as a mathematician for the US government department that later became NASA (National Aeronautics and Space Administration).

Katherine later worked on satellites, and on the Space Shuttle programme.

Space Shuttle

Mercury-Atlas 6

Mercury-Redstone 3

Apollo 11

Apollo 13

KATHERINE JOHNSON

American mathematician • 1918–2020

Reaching for the Moon

At NASA, Katherine was invited to work on complex projects to get spacecraft into Earth's orbit and beyond. Her calculations helped to launch the first American astronauts into space, to put the first humans on the Moon (and get them off again!), and to return the broken Apollo 13 spacecraft safely back to Earth. After she retired, Katherine was honoured with the Presidential Medal of Freedom. But, she said her greatest reward was the work itself — she loved going to work every single day.

> You tell me when you want it and where you want it to land, and I'll do it backwards and tell you when to take off.

Human computers

Along with Mary Jackson and Dorothy Vaughan, Katherine was part of a computing unit made up of brilliant African-American mathematicians, led by Dorothy. Their calculations, completed with paper and pen, made the first US space missions possible. Later, Mary became NASA's first Black female engineer.

Mary Jackson

Dorothy Vaughan

Materials scientists are explorers and inventors. They create advanced materials that help to make faster and more eco-friendly vehicles, longer-lasting batteries, more advanced computers, and better communication devices, such as mobile phones. Here are some world-changing materials and the problems they can solve — or cause.

Nanomaterials

Something extremely small, such as an atom, can be described as "nano". Graphene is just one atom thick, but incredibly strong. As well as being the lightest known nano material, it is also the best conductor of electricity.

Structure of graphene

This dress is made of graphene — however, nanomaterials are usua[lly] used for very small parts inside objects.

MATERIALS

New from old

"Rare-earth" metals were discovered hundreds of years ago, but are still being used to create new materials. They made many modern devices possible — for example, mobile phones vibrate using rare-earth neodymium magnets!

Tough ceramics

Everyday ceramics come in the form of plates and mugs. Yet, ceramics are also some of the toughest materials in the world. Silicon nitrides can keep their form in temperatures that would melt diamonds! They are used to make parts of machines that need to be very strong.

Velcro®, a fastener with tiny hooks that catch loops, was inspired by the hooks of natural burrs catching on a dog's coat.

Flexible laminate packaging is made from layers of plastic, paper, and metal.

Different types of synthetic rubber, which is used to make things such as tyres, are made from unique combinations of materials.

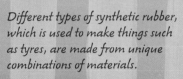

Mimicking nature

Nature is a great place to find ideas. Scientists try to copy features that help living things solve problems, such as the sticky pads that let lizards climb walls, and the way plants capture the Sun's energy.

The best of both

Composite materials combine two or more materials with different properties. For example, a light material and a strong material could make a strong, lightweight composite.

Strong, light carbon fibre (plastic and carbon) is great for racket frames.

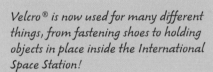

Velcro® is now used for many different things, from fastening shoes to holding objects in place inside the International Space Station!

Planet under pressure

Materials scientists have to be careful. Taking elements such as rare-earth metals from beneath the ground or ocean can damage the environment. Other materials that end up back in the soil, air, or water can harm wildlife.

Solving problems

New materials can solve problems. Plastic is cheap, light, and strong. However, it takes a very long time to break down, so plastic waste builds up. Scientists are trying to design types of plastic that are easier to reuse and recycle.

GLADYS WEST

American mathematician
1930–present

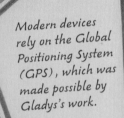

Modern devices rely on the Global Positioning System (GPS), which was made possible by Gladys's work.

Computers can speed up difficult calculations involving huge amounts of data, but only if someone has told them what to do! In the 1960s, the US Navy hired brilliant mathematicians, including Gladys West, to program some of the very first computers.

Gladys wrote software that told computers how to crunch the numbers and to help us understand all kinds of different things, including the strange paths of Neptune and Pluto around the Sun. But her most famous project focused on our own planet. The US Navy wanted to put satellites into orbit around the Earth to help ships find their way at sea. They would need to know exactly how far from the ground the satellites were.

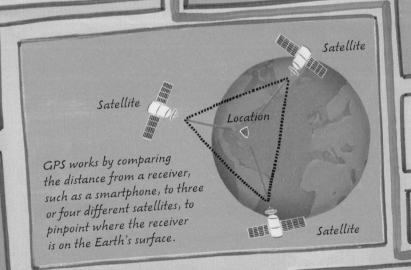

GPS works by comparing the distance from a receiver, such as a smartphone, to three or four different satellites, to pinpoint where the receiver is on the Earth's surface.

Wonky planet

The problem is, Earth has a very bumpy surface and is not a perfect sphere. For example, what counts as zero when we measure the height of a satellite in the sky? Should we use the top of the highest mountain or the bottom of the deepest ocean? What counts as sea level when tides are constantly rising and falling?

GPS uses a network of 24 satellites in total, each sending out signals at the same time. The time it takes a signal to reach your device tells the GPS how far you are from that satellite.

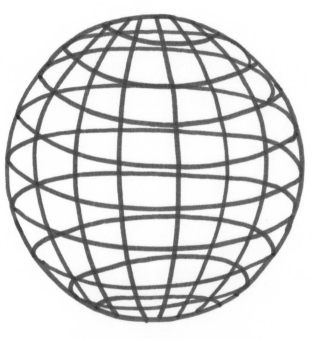

An ellipsoid is a mathematical model of the Earth that takes into account changes in altitude (height above sea level), gravity, and tides, and is simple and easy to use.

Gladys helped to solve this problem. She created software that taught the best computers of the time how to represent Earth's wonky shape as a simple mathematical model, called an ellipsoid. Using ellipsoids, computers can easily calculate the position of things on the Earth's surface, which is how GPS works today.

The geoid

For her work, Gladys had to understand the wonky shape of the Earth, called the geoid. She used data from satellites to build up an accurate picture of it.

SAU LAN WU

Chinese-American physicist
Early 1940s-present

Sau Lan Wu says that if something doesn't work out in life, you should never give up. Just keep going, and something else will come along and surprise you. This happened over and over again for Sau. She began life in poverty, sleeping at the back of a shop in a very poor area of Hong Kong. After finishing school, she applied to 50 US universities to study physics.

Only one offered her a place — but one was all that Sau needed! She was on her way to becoming a physicist.

Try to innovate.
Nothing will be easy.
But it is all worth
it to discover
something new.

Particles are boosted to almost the speed of light

Particle colliders
The particles that make up atoms are invisible to human senses. Physicists find out about them by smashing bigger particles together in an accelerator and analysing what happens.

The smallest things

Sau wanted to find out more about the building blocks of the Universe. At first, atoms were thought to be the particles that made up everything. Then scientists discovered atoms were made up of smaller particles, called protons, neutrons, and electrons. By the time Sau began her research, it was becoming clear that there were even smaller particles inside these. Sau helped to discover two of these — the J/psi particle and the gluon.

There are different types of particle – leptons, quarks, fermions, and bosons

Gluons help to hold quarks together to form bigger particles.

Without the Higgs boson, other particles would zoom around all over the place at the speed of light!

Sau helped to build the Standard Model – a list of the particles that make up everything, and the forces holding them together.

... and smashed together!

The collisions produce other particles, such as Higgs bosons, but they only exist for a split second.

The Large Hadron Collider is the world's largest particle collider. It's 27 km (17 miles) long, shaped like a huge ring, and is in Geneva, in Switzerland.

The J/psi particle was evidence for quarks – the building blocks of protons, neutrons, and electrons. This particle is made from smaller particles that are in the Standard Model.

Sau was also part of a huge team of scientists, who spent more than 30 years hunting for the final piece of the Standard Model. In 2012, experiments using the Large Hadron Collider detected the Higgs boson, a particle like no other.

Sau is still experimenting, but she has another big mission, too. She teaches physics students how to follow in her footsteps, ready to make the world-changing discoveries of the future.

FRANCISCA NNEKA OKEKE

Nigerian physicist • 1956–present

After leaving school, **Francisca worked** as a supply teacher, who filled in for other teachers when they were away. Francisca enjoyed setting and solving physics problems so much that she decided to study physics at university. This was not a popular choice for women at the time, but Francisca has helped to change this now.

Francisca became the first woman to lead the physics department at the University of Nigeria, and has mentored dozens of young scientists. She has shown them that physics is not a difficult subject, but a fun and practical way to find answers to interesting questions.

As a child, Francisca was fascinated by the changing sky. Why was it sometimes white, but sometimes blue? How did aeroplanes stay up? By asking questions and seeking answers, Francisca raced ahead in science and maths.

Secrets of the sky

The questions Francisca likes to solve focus on the strange happenings high in the Earth's atmosphere, and deep below its surface in the mantle and core. These layers of our planet are not visible to our eyes, but physicists can use instruments to collect data, then try to spot patterns to understand what's going on.

Francisca is particularly interested in an area of the atmosphere called the ionosphere. Her work has revealed more about how Earth's climate varies over time, which has helped us realise how the things we do can affect it.

Equatorial electrojet

The equatorial electrojet is a strong river of electrical current high above the Earth in the ionosphere. It's caused by solar activity in the ionosphere.

Ionosphere

The ionosphere is a thick layer of Earth's atmosphere, 50 to 1,000 km (30 to 620 miles) above the ground. It's important because the radio signals used by communication and navigation systems travel through it.

The Sun unleashes the solar wind — gusts of electrically charged particles, which zoom through space. Francisca has studied how this "space weather" affects the equatorial electrojet.

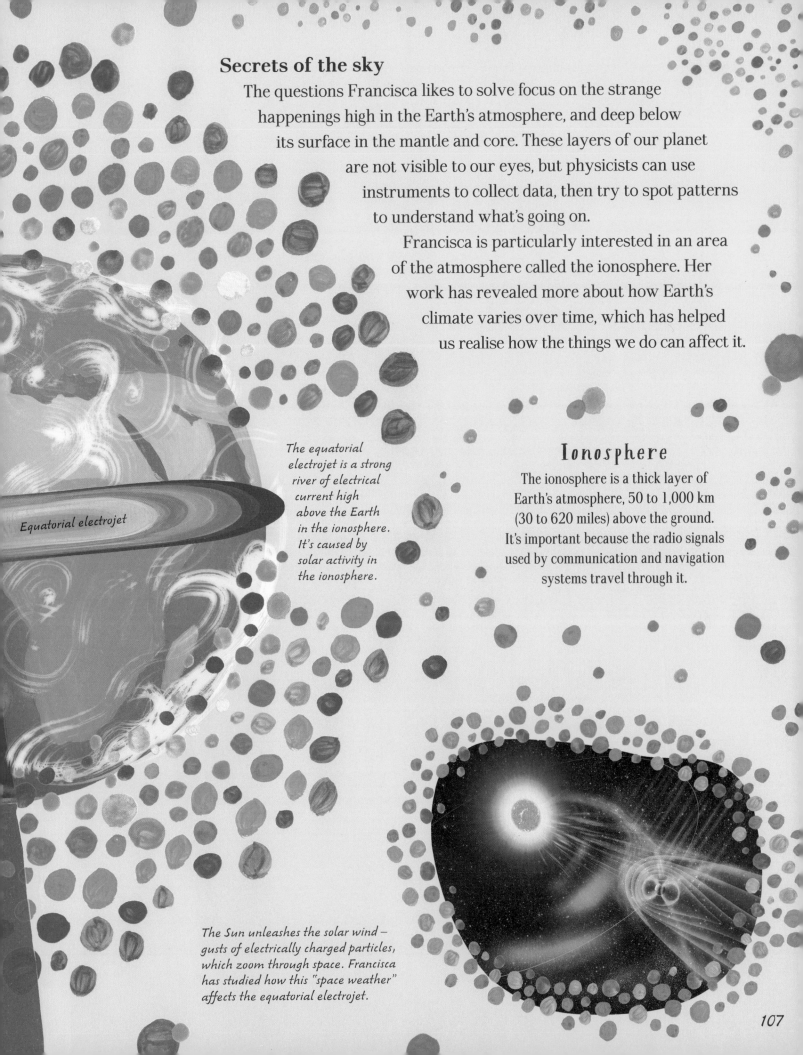

AMAZING
EARTH & SPACE

Earth and space scientists study changes that happen over billions of years, far beyond the scale and scope of a human life. To do this, they must piece together clues from ancient rocks and distant stars. The reward is understanding the strange structures of the Universe, including our very own special planet.

AGANICE OF THESSALY

Greek astronomer • c.3rd century BCE

Very little is known about **Aganice** of Thessaly, but historians have found clues that she was one of the first astronomers — scientists who study the night sky. Aganice lived around 2,000 years ago in Thessaly, in ancient Greece. She must have been very famous at the time, because she is mentioned in a book written more than 100 years after she lived. The author, Plutarch, said that Aganice understood lunar eclipses so well that she could predict them! However, he also hinted that Aganice didn't tell other people about the science behind her predictions.

Plutarch wrote that Aganice made people think that she could pull the Moon down from the sky! In ancient Greek times, many people would have found this terrifying. Stories linked the Moon with strange events and mythical creatures, such as werewolves.

Eclipses are named after the Greek word ekleipō, which means to disappear or cover up.

During a lunar eclipse, the full Moon changes colour as it moves into and out of Earth's shadow.

Lunar legacy

Of course, Aganice didn't really have magical powers. Just like today's scientists, she had learned that nature is not as chaotic as it seems. Aganice saw an order in things — the movements of the Sun, the Moon, stars, and planets follow rules, which make them predictable.

The ancient Greeks even created a device — called the Antikythera mechanism — to calculate positions of objects in the sky many years into the future. It is probably the oldest mechanical computer-like tool in the world. Devices like this may have helped Aganice to predict lunar eclipses, cycles the Moon still follows to this day.

The Aglaonice crater on Venus is named after Aganice.

There is a Greek saying: "Yes, as the Moon obeys Aganice", which means "That's for sure!"

Sun

Earth

Moon

Lunar eclipse

Total lunar eclipses happen when the Sun, the Earth, and the Moon are perfectly lined up in space, with the Earth in the middle. Our planet blocks most of the Sun's light from getting to the Moon. The little light that does get through makes the Moon look red or orange.

SHEN KUO
Chinese astronomer and mathematician
1031–1095

Specialist areas of science — such as geology, zoology, and palaeontology — are a recent invention. A thousand years ago, great thinkers didn't divide up knowledge in this way. They studied anything that interested them — and Shen Kuo was interested in everything!

Kuo began his career working for the Chinese government and excelled at every task he was given. For example, after solving an engineering problem to dredge (clear out) a canal, he discovered that the muck and silt being removed could be used to help crops to grow. Impressed by his work, the government gave Kuo more and more important jobs.

Kuo's books are the first to mention magnetic compasses. He wrote that they don't point to the true North (a fixed point) but to a magnetic North Pole.

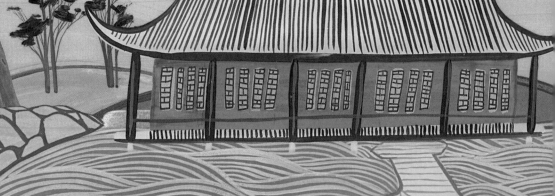

Kuo discovered seashell fossils up a mountain and realized that it must have once been beside the sea.

Kuo famously dreamed about a beautiful hillside — then was shocked to stumble across it in real life! He built a house there and called it Dream Pool.

Time to think

Kuo was brilliant at solving problems, but things didn't always go well. After working as a military leader, Kuo was blamed when 60,000 soldiers were killed by enemy forces. He was banished from the centre of government to a house he had built in the countryside.

For a deep thinker, this was bliss. Kuo happily began writing down all his scientific ideas about the world, creating a book called *Mengxi bitan* (Brush Talks from Dream Pool). It includes essays on dozens of different areas of nature — from the distant stars, to the rocks, animals, and plants he saw on his travels.

Many of Kuo's ideas were hundreds of years ahead of the rest of the world. For instance, he wrote about his worry that the environment was damaged when forests were cleared for wood to burn. Kuo's book is also the first to mention that the Earth's climate changes over time.

Board game genius

Maths-whizz Kuo worked out how many different combinations of counters are possible on an ancient board game called Go. He arrived at 10^{172}, which is 10 with 171 zeros after it! No one had ever calculated such a huge number before!

He found fossilized bamboo in an area where the weather meant bamboo couldn't grow. Kuo realized the climate had changed over time.

NASIR AL-DIN AL-TUSI

Persian philosopher, astronomer, and mathematician
1201–1274

Hundreds of years before Albert Einstein was born, the Islamic world already had a name that everyone knew meant genius — al-Tusi. When Nasir al-Din al-Tusi was just a boy, his dad passed away. It was his father's dying wish that Nasir would study hard.

Nasir did exactly that, and studied all kinds of different subjects, from mathematics and physics to philosophy and medicine. He was top of the class at everything! His wide-ranging talents led him to become an important figure in society who would be remembered for many hundreds of years.

Nasir's careful measurements helped him to accurately describe the circular movements of the planets in the night sky.

Nasir studied old texts and ideas — such as those of the ancient Greeks — and improved on them.

A library of ideas

Around 1220, Mongol forces invaded Nasir's homeland, led by their ruthless ruler, Genghis Khan. Nasir found safety at the fortress of Alamut, in modern-day Iran. He liked it there because it had a brilliant library where he could study. When Alamut was destroyed by the Mongols in 1256, Nasir was appointed their scientific advisor. He persuaded Genghis Khan's grandson, Hulegu, to build a huge observatory — a place where astronomers study space — in modern-day Azerbaijan.

Persian and Chinese astronomers worked side-by-side to build and operate instruments for measuring the movements of planets and stars. Nasir invented many of these instruments himself, too. The observatory became an important centre of learning, and was complete with another fantastic library.

Genghis Khan

At the fortress of Alamut, Nasir wrote about many topics, including ethics — the study of what is right and wrong.

Ever-changing animals

Nasir observed Earth just as carefully as space. He came up with a theory to explain how animals evolve, or change, over time. Adaptations he described include the long horns of the Persian gazelle and the sharp claws of a falcon.

Nasir created more than 160 books and papers, including important texts on astronomy, mathematics, and biology. For example, he wrote about the importance of trigonometry (the study of triangles) in answering huge mathematical problems. His questions and ideas inspired other scientists for centuries to come — in Islamic lands and far beyond.

Nasir's work may have inspired other scientists, such as Nicolaus Copernicus, hundreds of years later!

NICOLAUS COPERNICUS · 1473–1543

Polish astronomer

Nicolaus Copernicus was studying to become a priest, like his uncle, when he became fascinated by the movements of the stars and planets. Long before, ancient Greek astronomers had looked up and decided that the Sun, the Moon, and all the objects in the sky were orbiting, or moving around, the Earth. They believed that our planet was at the very centre of the Universe. This idea, called the geocentric model, remained for thousands of years. It was what Nicolaus had always been taught. However, as he looked up at the sky, he started to think that something entirely different was going on.

In old models, the constellations (groups of stars) are shown as the things they look like, such as animals. They were named after these things, in Latin.

In this image of the geocentric model, spheres show the Sun, the Moon, and planets, and symbols show the stars.

116

Have you noticed that Uranus and Neptune are missing from Nicolaus's model? It's because they hadn't been discovered yet!

Nicolaus released a book of his ideas just before he died. It didn't sell many copies at first!

112 Cn

The element Copernicium was named in honour of Nicolaus.

A model astronomer

Nicolaus worked out that the Earth was just another planet, orbiting the Sun. He created a new model of the Universe, called the heliocentric model. It put all the planets in the right order, and it even explained the seasons — more or less of the Sun's heat reaches different parts of the Earth during its orbit, causing hot and cold periods.

Nicolaus didn't share his theory for more than 35 years. There were things he couldn't understand, such as why the moving Earth feels so still underfoot. He didn't get everything right — for example, he believed the stars orbit the Sun, like the planets. But he helped turn astronomy into a studied science in which people question old ideas.

Finally we shall place the Sun himself at the centre of the Universe.

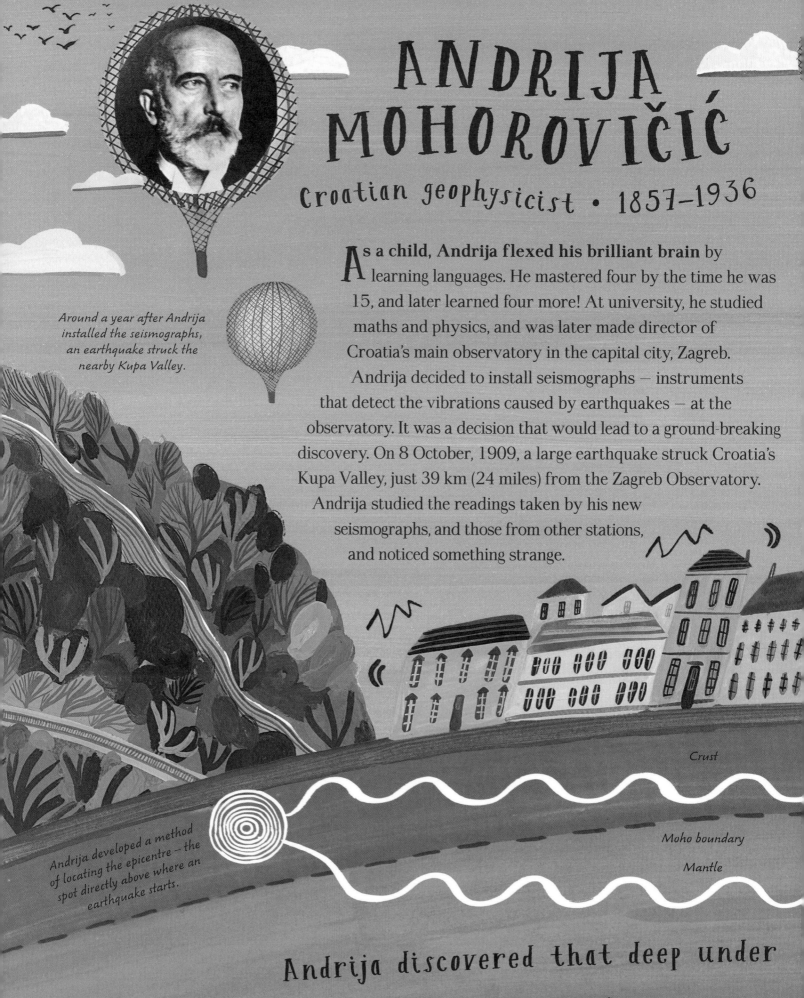

ANDRIJA MOHOROVIČIĆ

Croatian geophysicist • 1857–1936

Around a year after Andrija installed the seismographs, an earthquake struck the nearby Kupa Valley.

As a child, **Andrija flexed his brilliant brain** by learning languages. He mastered four by the time he was 15, and later learned four more! At university, he studied maths and physics, and was later made director of Croatia's main observatory in the capital city, Zagreb. Andrija decided to install seismographs — instruments that detect the vibrations caused by earthquakes — at the observatory. It was a decision that would lead to a ground-breaking discovery. On 8 October, 1909, a large earthquake struck Croatia's Kupa Valley, just 39 km (24 miles) from the Zagreb Observatory. Andrija studied the readings taken by his new seismographs, and those from other stations, and noticed something strange.

Andrija developed a method of locating the epicentre — the spot directly above where an earthquake starts.

Crust

Moho boundary

Mantle

Andrija discovered that deep under

Vibrations that shook the Earth

Some of the vibrations had arrived at Zagreb far sooner than expected. Somehow, they had sped up as they travelled deep underground! Andrija realized that the vibrations must have travelled through very different types of rock — an outer layer (now called the crust), and an inner layer where waves could travel much faster (now called the mantle). Andrija estimated that the Earth's crust is around 50 km (30 miles) thick. He was close to the truth — today's instruments show that the boundary between the crust and the mantle lies about 35 km (22 miles) underground. It has been named the Mohorovičić discontinuity, or "Moho" for short, in honour of the way Andrija's work completely changed the way we understand our planet.

Meteorology

At the beginning of his career, Andrija taught sailors about weather and ocean science at a nautical school. He was fascinated by ships because his father worked on a shipyard, so he had found a job that combined ships and science! Here, he set up his first weather station.

Andrija helped to persuade governments to build earthquake-proof buildings.

The top two layers of rock were later named the crust and mantle. The boundary between them was named after Andrija.

Vibrations travelling through the mantle reached Zagreb first.

the ground lie different layers of rock.

Alfred Wegener began his science career as an astronomer, staring into space. However, he soon became more interested in the fascinating things he saw on our own planet.

Alfred became a professor of Earth sciences, seeking to understand our planet inside and out. One of the strangest things he noticed was how well the coastlines of North America and South America matched up with the coastlines of Europe and Africa, like pieces of a giant jigsaw. Alfred was also amazed to learn that the fossils of similar animals had been found on opposite sides of the huge Atlantic Ocean.

Other scientists had thought that this was because ancient animals had crossed "land bridges", which once connected the continents. But, Alfred had a theory — it wasn't the animals that had moved, it was the continents themselves!

Fossils of Mesosaurus, an ancient reptile, have been found far away from each other – in both southern Africa and South America.

NORTH AMERICA

Atlantic Ocean

SOUTH AMERICA

ALFRED WEGENER

Gerﾏan meteorologist, geophysicist, and polar explorer • 1880–1930

Continental drift

The Earth once had just one huge land mass, which Alfred named Pangaea (meaning "all lands"). Over time, Pangaea split up into pieces. These drifted apart into the continents we live on today, which are still moving very slowly!

270 million years ago

200 million years ago

EUROPE

AFRICA

Alfred noticed that the shape of the coastlines of Africa and South America appeared to be able to slot together.

Proof of Pangaea

Alfred collected masses of evidence to support his idea. He used fossils and rocks to show that parts of the world had completely different climates than they do today because the continents used to be in different places. However, there was one thing Alfred couldn't explain — *how* could something as large as a continent possibly move around?

Alfred lived for adventure and loved hiking, sailing, and exploring. He even broke a world record by floating in a hot-air balloon for 52 hours!

Sadly, few people took Alfred's idea seriously while he was alive. But, 20 years after he died, new discoveries began to prove him right. As technology allowed us to explore the deepest oceans, evidence was found showing that the Earth's crust is split into huge pieces, called tectonic plates, which move around very slowly. These movements carry continents with them — just as Alfred said!

Alfred died while hiking across Greenland on a heroic rescue mission.

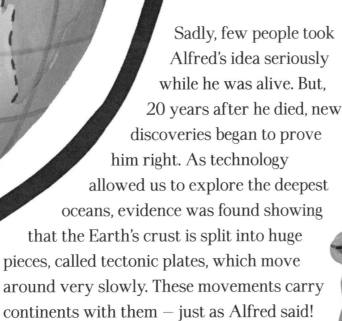

SEEING THE UNSEEABLE

Instruments help scientists gather information about amazing things that we cannot see, hear, smell, taste, or feel with our senses. Thanks to these tools and techniques, we can peer inside planets and deep into space. We can observe particles too tiny to see and even look back in time!

Parker Solar Probe

Space probes contain lots of instruments for exploring places too difficult to visit in person. This rocket sent the Parker Solar Probe hurtling deep into the scorching atmosphere of the Sun itself.

Magnetic field

Geophysicists use instruments to measure the Earth's magnetic field. It is not steady, but varies across space and time. Understanding it is important for navigation, plotting maps, and detecting minerals deep under the ground.

Atmospheric radar dish

By bouncing radio waves off an object, radar systems can tell us its shape, speed, and direction of travel. This huge dish is part of a radar system that monitors storms and other weather in the Earth's atmosphere.

Ice core

The deepest layers of ice that cover Antarctica and Greenland are hundreds of thousands of years old. By drilling down and taking pieces out of this ice, scientists can obtain trapped bubbles of ancient air. This tells us what the climate was like in the past.

New Horizons

In 2015, the New Horizons probe became the first spacecraft to closely explore Pluto, a dwarf planet beyond all the planets in the Solar System. It sent back incredible photographs of the surface.

Chang'e 4 Moon lander

Moon lander

Landers are robots designed to land on the surface of planets, moons, asteroids, and comets. They are packed with instruments that only work close-up to an object. This lunar lander touched down on the Earth's Moon in 2019.

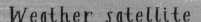

Weather satellite

A huge network of satellites monitors the Earth's weather and climate from positions high above the planet. They use radar, cameras, and other tools to do this.

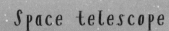

James Webb Space Telescope

Space telescope

Telescopes placed in orbit around the Earth get a better view of space. The light and other radiation they collect hasn't had to travel through the Earth's atmosphere first.

Seismometer

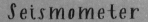

Seismometers detect vibrations of the ground, including movements too small for us to feel. They can tell us about earthquakes and volcanic explosions, but also provide clues about what the Earth is like deep underground.

What can't be measured?

One problem in science is that we can only observe things that our senses or instruments can detect. This adds up to less than 5 per cent of the Universe! The stuff we can't detect yet is known as dark matter and dark energy.

EDWIN HUBBLE

American cosmologist
1889–1953

Edwin fell in love with science as a student. However, Edwin's father didn't know anything about physics and was worried. He wanted Edwin to become a lawyer. Edwin followed his father's wishes and studied law, but he couldn't stop thinking about physics. He went on to do a second graduate degree in astronomy, using a telescope to take photographs of strange clusters of stars known as nebulae.

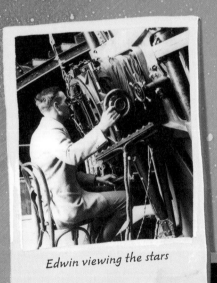

Edwin viewing the stars

The Mount Wilson Observatory

Edwin was offered a job at the Mount Wilson Observatory in California, USA, where the world's most powerful telescope, the 100-inch Telescope, was being built. Edwin joined the US Army to fight in World War II, but afterwards he returned to gaze at the stars.

The 100-inch Telescope

Spiral galaxy

Elliptical galaxy

Irregular galaxy

Edwin studied lots of spiral nebulae – and found that they were part of distant galaxies. Astronomers could now agree that the Universe was made up of many galaxies, of different shapes and sizes.

Galaxies far, far away

The telescope at the Mount Wilson Observatory gave Edwin a much better view of the mysterious nebulae. He was particularly interested in nebulae shaped liked spirals. At that time, the only galaxy astronomers knew about was our own – the Milky Way. Were nebulae clusters of stars within the Milky Way? Or could they be distant galaxies themselves?

Peering at a spiral nebula known as Andromeda, Edwin noticed that some stars changed in brightness. He worked out that less-bright stars were further away, and he used this knowledge to calculate the distance of different stars from the Earth. The distance turned out to be enormous – at least three times further than the outer limits of the Milky Way! This proved that Andromeda was a galaxy itself.

Edwin taught us how to unlock the secrets of space beyond our own galaxy.

Edwin discovered how changes in the colour of light from distant stars and galaxies can tell us how far they are from the Earth.

The first telescope in space was named "Hubble" after Edwin.

125

CECILIA PAYNE–GAPOSCHKIN

British–American astronomer
1900–1979

Our nearest star – the Sun – is an unimaginable 150 million km (93 million miles) away. Today's spacecraft cannot get much closer than 11 million km (7 million miles) to it without melting. Yet we've known for almost 100 years what this fiery star is made of. Cecilia Payne-Gaposchkin was the star scientist who solved this puzzle.

Cecilia worked out the Sun's secrets from Earth, using special photographs of stars, called spectra. These photographs split the white light from a star into the rainbow of different colours of light that it's made from. Cecilia found a new way to read these spectra.

As a child, Cecilia spent hours in the library exploring her favourite subjects: science and mathematics.

These dark lines, known as Fraunhofer lines, show different colours that are missing from this spectrum. The missing colours can be used to figure out which elements are present in the spectrum.

This missing colour has been absorbed by hydrogen.

This missing colour has been absorbed by iron.

Cecilia explained how the mixture of different colours of light given out by a star tells us the temperature at its fiery surface.

Hydrogen and helium

For years, scientists had looked at the spectrum of light from the Sun and decided that it was made of the same stuff as the Earth — including mostly heavy elements, such as iron and calcium. Other stars had different spectra, so scientists assumed they must be made of different elements. Cecilia realized this was wrong.

Cecilia discovered that the differences between light spectra from different stars were not due to different ingredients, but different temperatures. She also came up with a way to calculate how much of each element was present in a spectrum. Cecilia was surprised to discover that the Sun is mainly made of hydrogen and a little bit of helium. She shared her breakthrough with other leading astronomers. At first, they said that this was impossible. But gradually, Cecilia was proven right — our understanding of stars and the Universe had changed forever.

Cecilia had to battle for recognition, but eventually became Harvard's first female professor and head of the astronomy department.

Solar spectrum

Sunlight looks white, but it is really a mixture of many colours. A spectrum looks a bit like a colourful barcode, where each dark line shows us a specific colour of light that is missing. These colours are missing because they have been absorbed by elements in the star's atmosphere. If we know which colours of light are absorbed by which elements, we can work out what elements make up a specific star.

This missing colour has been absorbed by oxygen.

127

L'UDMILA PAJDUŠÁKOVÁ

Slovak astronomer
1916–1979

L'udmila Pajdušáková began her career as an observatory technician. As she set up and mended equipment, and helped astronomers analyse their observations, L'udmila became fascinated by the meteors and comets that could be spotted streaking across the night sky. She started studying astronomy in her spare time and became the first female astronomer in her country.

World War II had recently ended, and governments around the world were now racing to explore space. L'udmila and her team of four other astronomers earned funding for a careful comet-hunting mission. For years, they spent their nights taking it in turns to search the sky.

L'udmila's comets were discovered using a pair of giant binoculars rather than a telescope!

The Skalnaté Pleso Observatory is high in the mountains, where the skies are dark and clear.

128

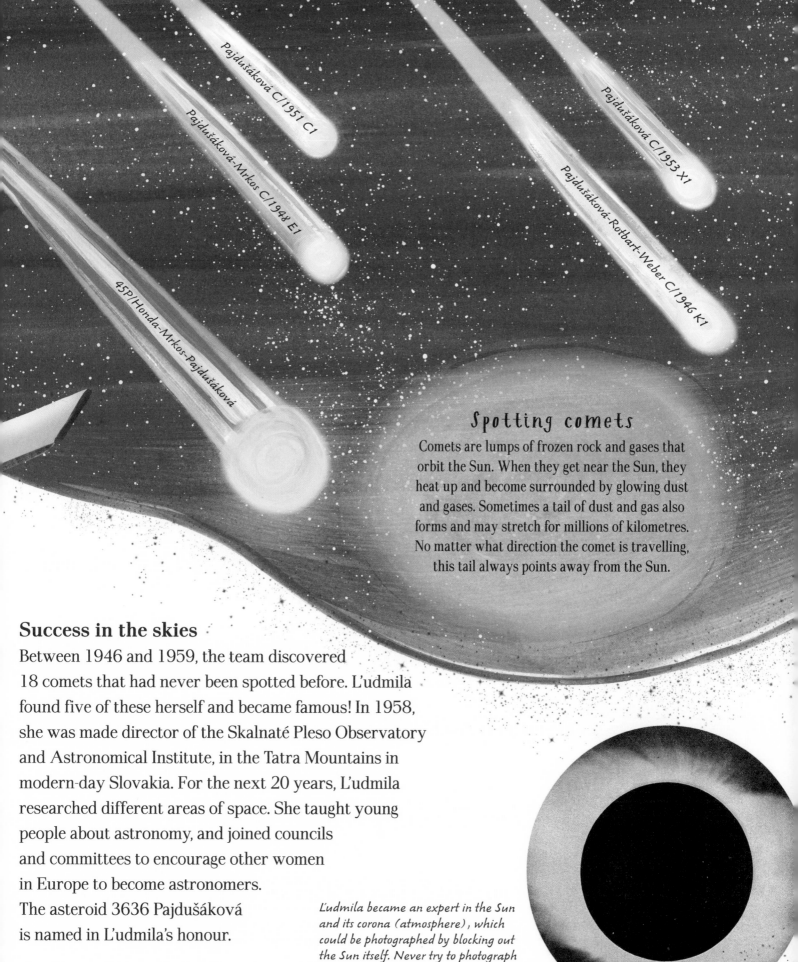

Pajdušáková C/1951 C1

Pajdušáková-Mrkos C/1948 E1

45P/Honda-Mrkos-Pajdušáková

Pajdušáková C/1953 X1

Pajdušáková-Rotbart-Weber C/1946 K1

Spotting comets

Comets are lumps of frozen rock and gases that orbit the Sun. When they get near the Sun, they heat up and become surrounded by glowing dust and gases. Sometimes a tail of dust and gas also forms and may stretch for millions of kilometres. No matter what direction the comet is travelling, this tail always points away from the Sun.

Success in the skies

Between 1946 and 1959, the team discovered 18 comets that had never been spotted before. L'udmila found five of these herself and became famous! In 1958, she was made director of the Skalnaté Pleso Observatory and Astronomical Institute, in the Tatra Mountains in modern-day Slovakia. For the next 20 years, L'udmila researched different areas of space. She taught young people about astronomy, and joined councils and committees to encourage other women in Europe to become astronomers. The asteroid 3636 Pajdušáková is named in L'udmila's honour.

L'udmila became an expert in the Sun and its corona (atmosphere), which could be photographed by blocking out the Sun itself. Never try to photograph the Sun yourself, as this would damage your eyes and could cause blindness.

129

KATIA & MAURICE KRAFFT
French volcanologists
1942–1991 & 1946–1991

Explosive eruptions of hot gas, ash, and lava make volcanoes some of the most dangerous places on the planet. However, for both Katia and Maurice Krafft, it was love at first sight! As a child, Katia was captivated by films about the fiery forces that shape the Earth. For Maurice, one glimpse of a real-life volcano made him determined to study geology (the science of the Earth itself).

Stromboli, Italy

Katia and Maurice's careers began with a trip to Stromboli, an active island volcano in Italy.

Eldfell, Iceland

Katia and Maurice became famous for the daring risks they took to capture eruptions on camera, including Eldfell in 1973.

Katia and Maurice met at university and soon arranged to visit an active volcano together – Stromboli, in Italy. Every few minutes, Stromboli belched out ash, bits of glowing lava, and lumps of stone. The couple returned from the trip with amazing photographs. They realized they could sell photographs and films to fund a life of visiting volcanoes!

Hot rod

Protective suit

Heat-resistant gloves

Volcano kit

Safety gear, such as silver, protective suits that reflect the intense heat from volcanoes, can only protect volcanologists from some of the dangers. They need to be careful and prepared for anything when working.

A life of lava

For the next 25 years, this is exactly what Katia and Maurice did. Together, they travelled all over the world and climbed around half of the world's active volcanoes. In a time before robots and drones, they were able to see and record incredible scenes of lava flows, pyroclastic debris, and volcanic craters. They created a huge collection of videos and more than 300,000 photographs, which could be used in films, books, and documentaries.

Katia and Maurice became the most well-known volcanologists in the world. Each adventure paid for the next one, but their work also helped to teach governments how to keep communities safe near volcanoes, and inspired new generations of volcanologists.

A pyroclastic flow is a glowing cloud of superheated gas, ash, and rocks, which moves downhill very quickly.

Mount Unzen, Japan

Along with more than 50 others, Katia and Maurice were killed by a pyroclastic flow while visiting Mount Unzen as it erupted in 1991.

New land is formed as the lava cools.

Above ground the molten rock is called lava.

A volcano is a place where molten rock, ash, and gases escape from beneath the Earth's surface.

Studying volcanoes helps scientists to predict eruptions.

Deep underground the molten rock is called magma.

131

STEPHEN HAWKING

British theoretical physicist
1942–2018

Stephen Hawking used his brilliant brain to explore space and time, and he helped millions of people to understand the Universe better. For most of his life, Stephen lived with a condition called motor neurone disease. This slowly stopped his body from working. But, no matter how challenging life became, Stephen kept asking questions and seeking answers as a theoretical physicist.

Stephen didn't carry out experiments or peer through telescopes. Instead, he explored the Universe in his mind, and tried to describe it using mathematics. This allowed Stephen to make predictions about things that no one had ever seen, such as black holes.

Stephen (in white) studied at both the University of Oxford and the University of Cambridge, in the UK.

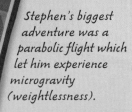

Stephen's biggest adventure was a parabolic flight which let him experience microgravity (weightlessness).

Hawking radiation

Stephen combined Albert Einstein's ideas about gravity with quantum theory to understand black holes better. His calculations showed that some radiation *can* escape from a black hole, so over time the old star will evaporate and disappear!

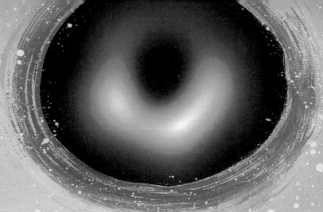

This is the first-ever photograph of a black hole. It was taken in 2019.

Black holes are areas of space with such strong gravity that nothing seems to escape — not even light.

Black holes and beyond

As a massive star runs out of fuel, the nuclear reactions deep inside slow down. There is nothing to balance the star's huge gravitational pull, so the star collapses and all of its mass gets packed into a tiny lump. It was thought that the gravity around this lump is so incredibly strong that nothing can escape it — not even light! However, Stephen disproved this when he showed that *some* radiation can escape a black hole. Stephen visited black holes in his mind, using maths to work out what we may find there. He became known for his incredible scientific brain, but also for his talent at communicating science through books and talks.

When motor neurone disease made it impossible for Stephen to speak, he began using a voice synthesizer. His electronic voice became famous around the world.

Black holes form when massive stars run out of fuel.

Be curious. [...] Unleash your imagination. Shape the future.

NEIL deGRASSE TYSON

American astrophysicist and science communicator • 1958–present

When Neil deGrasse Tyson was nine years old, he visited the Hayden Planetarium in New York City, USA, for the first time. A planetarium is a theatre that is built to share the wonders of the night sky. Instead of looking across at a stage, the audience gazes up at pictures projected on a curved ceiling. As Neil looked up at the starry dome, he was full of amazement and bursting with questions. He studied physics and astronomy, and then trained as an astrophysicist, using his mind to explore the Universe far beyond where we can possibly travel.

Neil completed several university degrees in the 1980s, and did valuable research to help us understand more about the structure of galaxies, and the way stars form and die over time. His work was so impressive that in 1996, Neil got his dream job, as director of the Hayden Planetarium itself.

Millions of people learned more about the Universe thanks to Neil's film, Cosmos: A Spacetime Odyssey.

Hayden Planetarium

The globe-shaped theatre inside this glass building is the Hayden Planetarium. Thousands of people visit it every year, to see incredible shows exploring distant planets, stars, and galaxies.

Space storyteller

Neil is not just a talented scientist, but also a great science communicator. He loves inspiring people who haven't studied science to find out more about the Universe and everything in it — from the largest stars to the smallest life forms that may exist somewhere in space. Neil began by writing magazine articles and books, and has since presented hugely popular shows on radio and television. He has won many awards for his work, and has been honoured in space as well as on Earth — with an asteroid named 13123 Tyson.

> Knowing where you came from is no less important than knowing where you are going.

135

MORE SCIENTISTS

Maggie Aderin-Pocock
1968–present

Space scientist Maggie designed instruments to orbit the Earth onboard the James Webb Space Telescope. She is also a well-known science communicator who shares the wonders of space with millions of people on television.

Frederick Banting
1891–1941

A disease called diabetes was very difficult to treat before Canadian scientist Frederick and his assistant discovered insulin, in 1921. This hormone is produced by the pancreas of people without diabetes, and it can be made outside the body and used to control blood sugar.

Ben Barres
1954–2017

Ben's work showed how mysterious cells called glia are an essential part of our brain – they help nerves to grow and make connections. Ben was a transgender man, and became an inspirational role model for LGBTQ+ scientists.

Robert Boyle
1627–1691

Boyle's Law is Robert's famous description of how squeezing a gas changes the space that it takes up. His careful experiments helped him make dozens of other discoveries, too, in physics, medicine, Earth sciences, and chemistry.

Sigmund Freud
1856–1939

The research of Austrian neurologist Sigmund completely changed the way people understood human behaviour. His ideas about how the human brain worked also helped him to invent a new type of therapy, called psychoanalysis.

Margherita Hack
1922–2013

Italian astrophysicist Margherita studied stars and their atmospheres. She transformed an observatory in Italy into a world-leading research centre that helped to plan one of the most productive satellites ever launched – the International Ultraviolet Explorer.

Edmond Halley
1656–1742

Edmond was the first astronomer to catalogue the stars visible from the Southern Hemisphere (half of the Earth south of the Equator). But, he is most famous for proving that three comets spotted in 1531, 1607, and 1682 were the same comet, now called Halley's Comet.

Alma Levant Hayden
1927–1967

Alma was one of the first African-American scientists to work for the US government. She was talented at using a technique called spectrophotometry to identify different chemicals. In one famous case, she proved that a supposed cure for cancer was really a fraud.

Alexa Canady
1950–present

As the first African-American woman to become a neurosurgeon in the USA, Alexa smashed down barriers in science and medicine. She became chief of neurosurgery at a children's hospital, helping hundreds of young patients.

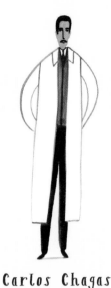

Carlos Chagas
1879–1934

Brazilian doctor Carlos discovered the microscopic parasite that causes a deadly illness now known as Chagas disease. He showed how insects passed it from person to person. Importantly, he also described how tackling poverty could stop the disease from spreading.

Annie Easley
1933–2011

Annie began her career as a human computer at NASA. At first, she did complex calculations by hand. As technology changed, she became a brilliant computer scientist, writing programs that made new types of power technology possible.

Lloyd Noel Ferguson
1918–2011

As a biochemist, Lloyd researched the carbon-based molecules that make up all living things, revealing strange secrets behind our sense of taste. Lloyd was also a brilliant teacher, helping hundreds of Black students to get started in chemistry.

Robert Hooke
1635–1703

Robert made incredible discoveries in many areas of science, from the rotation of planets to the structure of snowflakes. He came up with the word "cell" and discovered Hooke's Law, which predicts how much a material will be stretched by a given force.

Muhammad ibn Zakariya al-Razi
854–925 CE

Many discoveries about the way our bodies work can be traced back to this genius Persian doctor. He wrote more than 220 books about medicine and chemistry, all while running a busy hospital!

Hans Krebs
1900–1981

Hans shared the 1953 Nobel Prize in Physiology or Medicine for his discovery of an important series of chemical reactions that allow living things to release energy from their food. This process is known as the Krebs cycle.

Wangari Muta Maathai
1940–2011

Wangari was a biologist who founded the Green Belt Movement, which tries to stop deforestation. It led to more than 30 million trees being planted. Wangari became Kenya's first female professor and the first African woman to win a Nobel Prize.

Ettore Majorana
1906–?

Italian Ettore was a young scientist using his brilliant mind to understand atoms, when he suddenly vanished in 1938. The mystery has never been solved. Had he kept working, many physicists think he could have made world-changing discoveries, like Isaac Newton or Albert Einstein.

Julie Makani
1970–present

An award-winning medical researcher in Tanzania, Julie works to make blood disorders better. She leads efforts to turn research into health policies and practices that improve the lives of patients living with a blood disorder called sickle cell disease.

Barbara McClintock
1902–1992

Barbara helped us to understand what genes are and how they work. She proved that a genome (all genetic material of a living thing) is not fixed like beads on a string, but constantly being rearranged. This began a new field of science called cytogenetics, and won Barbara a Nobel Prize.

Mario J. Molina
1943–2020

Along with another scientist, Mexican chemist Mario showed how certain gases, called chlorofluorocarbons (CFCs), lead to the destruction of the ozone layer that protects the Earth from harmful solar radiation. Mario worked tirelessly to get CFCs banned from everyday use.

Leopold Ružička
1887–1976

Leopold studied the remarkable substances found in nature. He helped perfume makers put science into practice by making artificial versions of chemicals with strong smells. He later discovered how to produce important hormones that act as messengers in our bodies.

Katsuko Saruhashi
1920–2007

Raindrops falling down a window triggered Katsuko's curiosity about the science of our planet. She became a celebrated geoscientist, who warned the world that testing nuclear weapons above ground polluted the Earth's air and oceans.

Ignaz Semmelweis
1818–1865

Ignaz was a Hungarian doctor who worked out that doctors were accidentally spreading infections in hospitals. By insisting that doctors wash their hands after treating each patient, Ignaz showed how bacterial infection could be controlled and prevented.

Helen Taussig
1898–1986

A learning difficulty called dyslexia, with which some people may find it harder than others to read and write, didn't stop Helen becoming a brilliant doctor. She helped to develop an operation to correct a heart defect, which stops some newborn babies from getting enough oxygen.

Ellen Ochoa
1958–present

Ellen's skills as an engineer took her all the way into space. After four exciting space missions, and completing almost 1,000 hours in orbit, she worked for NASA, becoming director of the Johnson Space Center.

Max Planck
1858–1947

Quantum theory is a set of ideas and laws that helps physicists describe and predict the behaviour of the smallest particles in the Universe. German physicist Max developed quantum theory in the early 1900s. Since then, it has led to discoveries and inventions that have changed the world.

Claudius Ptolemy
100–c.170 CE

For 1,400 years, the science of astronomy was based entirely on the ideas of the Egyptian scientist Ptolemy! His model of how the Sun, the Moon, and the planets orbit Earth turned out to be wrong, but it is important in understanding the history of science.

Sally Ride
1951–2012

Sally was a physicist and the first American woman to travel into space. She got the job after NASA advertised for young scientists to train as astronauts. During two missions, Sally conducted dozens of different experiments, spending just over two weeks in space.

Mashudu Tshifularo
1964–present

In 1995, Mashudu became the first Black ear, nose and throat professor in South Africa. He later pioneered a new technique in ear surgery, using tiny replacement bones that had been made using 3D printing technology.

Irene Uchida
1917–2013

Canadian scientist Irene built a huge genetic database of twins who were happy to help with research, allowing both her and other scientists to make important genetic discoveries. Studying the similarities and differences between the genes of twins helps medical researchers understand conditions that have a genetic cause.

Ian Wilmut
1944–present

As a young biologist, Ian worked on genetic modification of animals to produce useful medicines. He is famous for leading the team who were the first to clone a mammal – a sheep named Dolly. Today, Ian works on improving the cloning of stem cells for medicine.

Shinya Yamanaka
1962–present

Stem cells promise to help us produce new types of medical treatment. Japanese researcher Shinya made a Nobel Prize-winning breakthrough when he developed a way of reprogramming ordinary body cells to turn them into stem cells.

GLOSSARY

adaptation
When an animal or plant changes over time, helping it to survive in its habitat

agronomist
Scientist who studies harvesting and growing crops

astronomy
Study of the Universe, including space, galaxies, and solar systems

atom
Smallest unit of an element. It contains protons, neutrons, and electrons

atomic number
Number of protons in an element's atom

bacteria
Tiny living things. Some bacteria can cause diseases

biology
Branch of science concerned with life and living things

characteristics
Features of something, such as the seed colour of pea plants

chemistry
Branch of science concerned with substances and how they react with each other

climate
Weather patterns for a particular area over time

continent
Large area of land, such as Europe or Africa

decay
Process of radioactive atoms breaking apart

DNA
Chemical that genes are made of. Stands for deoxyribonucleic acid

element
Simplest substance, with one type of atom. There are more than 100 different elements and they include hydrogen, carbon, oxygen, and gold

epidemic
Large outbreak of a disease

evolution
Gradual changes in living things over a long period of time, so that they adapt to their environment

expedition
Trip taken to explore unknown lands

extinct
When a species of animal or plant has completely died out

fossil fuel
Fuel made from plants and animals that died millions of years ago. Fossil fuels include gas, oil, and coal

genes
Coded sections of DNA. They control the way living things work and develop

genetics
Study of genes

gravity
Invisible force of attraction between two objects, such as the pull between Earth and the Moon

habitat
Place where a species of animal or plant lives

hybrid
When two things are combined to make something new

laboratory
Room in which scientific experiments are performed. Often shortened to "lab"

magnetic
Used to describe magnets, which are objects that attract some substances such as the metal iron with an invisible force

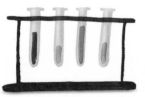

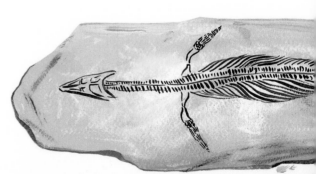

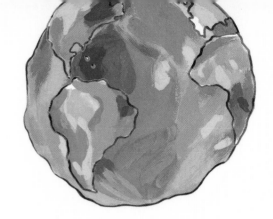

meteorologist
Scientist who studies the Earth's atmosphere and weather

microbe
Any living thing too small to see without using a microscope

molecule
Two or more atoms (tiny particles of a chemical element) bonded together

NASA
US government agency responsible for space missions and space-related research. Stands for National Aeronautic and Space Administration

naturalist
Someone who likes to observe or study living things in their natural environment

nuclear energy
Energy that is released when breaking the centre of atoms apart

observatory
Place where astronomers study space

palaeontologist
Scientist who studies fossils

Pangaea
Supercontinent that was formed from all of Earth's continents. It existed hundreds of millions of years ago, and broke apart to form the continents we know today

particle
Very tiny part of something, even smaller than an atom

physics
Branch of science concerned with matter, movement, forces, and energy

pyroclastic flow
Eruption of hot gas, rocks, and ash that moves rapidly down a volcano's slopes

radiation
Movement of energy in the form of waves or particles. Sunlight, X-rays, and radio waves are all types of radiation. Some types can be harmful to living things

refraction
When light waves bend as they pass through a transparent object, such as a glass prism or window

scholar
Person who is an expert on a subject

species
Group of similar living animals or plants. Members of the same species look similar, and can breed together to produce offspring

tectonic plate
Large, slow-moving piece of the Earth's crust

theorem
Statement in science that can be proved to be true

transform
To change or convert into something else

vaccination
Medicine that teaches the body how to fight off an infection

volcanologist
Scientist who studies volcanoes

X-ray
Invisible beams of light that pass through soft tissue, such as skin, but are soaked up by thicker tissue, such as bone

zoology
Study of animals

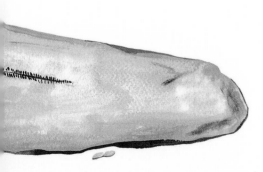

INDEX

ACKNOWLEDGEMENTS

About the author

Isabel Thomas is an award-winning science writer and author of a galaxy of books for young audiences. She studied Human Sciences at the University of Oxford, so writing about people in science is her dream job! Isabel lives in Cambridge, in the UK, with three children (who are guinea pigs for her books and activities) and two actual guinea pigs (who are no help whatsoever).

About the illustrator

Jessamy Hawke has been drawing since she was old enough to hold a pencil. She lives between London and Dorset, in the UK, where she enjoys walking along the coast and finding spots to sit and paint outdoors. Jessamy also illustrated *Explorers* and *Inventors*, other DK children's books. When she's in the studio, she's kept company by her dog, Mortimer, and her two cats, Marcel and Rhubarb.

About the consultants

Dr Stephen Haddelsey is a British historian and the author of seven books; he has also edited three historical manuscripts for their first publication. He is a Fellow of both the Royal Geographical Society and the Royal Historical Society, and an Honorary Research Fellow at the University of East Anglia.

Lisa Burke has been writing and consulting on science books for DK since 2005. She studied Natural Sciences at Cambridge University, then went on to work at Sky News as a presenter, weather forecaster, and science correspondent. She created the news platform RTL Today, and now lives in Luxembourg, where she works as a broadcaster across a range of different media, but always loves to promote science where possible.

DK would like to thank: Syed Md Farhan and Vijay Kandwal for cut-outs; Steve Crozier for repro work; Polly Goodman for proofreading; Helen Peters for the index; Bianca Hezekiah for her insightful comments; and Tony Stevens of Disability Rights UK for his comments on the book.

Picture Credits

The publisher would like to thank the following for their kind permission to reproduce their photographs:

(Key: a-above; b-below/bottom; c-centre; f-far; l-left; r-right; t-top)

8 **Alamy Stock Photo:** Axis Images (tr); The Natural History Museum, London (bc); PhotoStock-Israel (br). 9 **Alamy Stock Photo:** imageBROKER / Silvana Guilhermino (br). **Dreamstime.com:** Colin Moore (tl). 10 **Alamy Stock Photo:** Pictorial Press Ltd (tl). 11 **Alamy Stock Photo:** Morley Read (cr). **Getty Images / iStock:** wwing (cra). 12 **Alamy Stock Photo:** FLHC A22 (tl); Martin Shields (cb). 14 **Alamy Stock Photo:** AAA Collection (cr); GL Archive (tl); Eng Wah Teo (bc). **The Trustees of the Natural History Museum, London:** Collected in the Amazon by Alfred Russel Wallace between 1848-1852 (bl). 15 **Alamy Stock Photo:** Pictorial Press Ltd (cb); The Natural History Museum, London (clb). **Getty Images / iStock:** Grafissimo (tc). **Science Photo Library:** Paul D Stewart (cr). 16 **Alamy Stock Photo:** ARCHIVIO GBB (tl); WILDLIFE GmbH (clb). **Science Photo Library:** Steve Gschmeissner (tr). 18 **Alamy Stock Photo:** World History Archive (tl). **Dreamstime.com:** Nazar Nazaruk (bc); Tashka2000 (bl). 20 **Alamy Stock Photo:** Sunda Island Pit Viper (tl). 21 **SuperStock:** View Pictures Ltd (tl). 22 **Alamy Stock Photo:** Science History Images / Photo Researchers (tl). 23 **Alamy Stock Photo:** Universal Art Archive (tr). **Getty Images:** The LIFE Picture Collection / Alfred Eisenstaedt (tc); The LIFE Picture Collection / George Silk (crb). 24 **Albanian Authority of Files:** Sabina Kasimati and Elsa Kasimati (tl) **Alamy Stock Photo:** Nature Photographers Ltd / Paul R. Sterry (tr). **Dreamstime.com:** Goruppa (cla); Mirkorosenau (br). 25 **Dreamstime.com:** Alexander Raths (br). **Getty Images / iStock:** abadonian (cla). 26 **Alamy Stock Photo:** Pictorial Press Ltd (tl). **Science Photo Library:** (bl). 27 **Getty Images:** Bettmann (tl, cra). 28 **Dreamstime.com:** Olja Simovic (bc). **Getty Images:** Tetra Images (clb). **Getty Images / iStock:** Vladimir Zapletin (crb). **Science Photo Library:** A. Barrington Brown, © Gonville & Caius College (cra). 29 **Dreamstime.com:** Sarah Marchant (tr). **Science Photo Library:** David Parker (cb). 30 **Getty Images:** Toronto Star / Keith Beaty (tl). 31 **Alamy Stock Photo:** Science History Images / Photo Researchers (cra). **Dreamstime.com:** Grieze (tr). 32 **Alamy Stock Photo:** Imaginechina Limited (tr). 33 **Alamy Stock Photo:** Xinhua / Ding Lei (cr). 34 **Getty Images:** United News / Popperfoto (tl). 35 **Alamy Stock Photo:** Everett Collection, Inc. / © Universal (cr); Liam White (tc, br). 36 **Getty Images:** Corbis Historical / Paulo Fridman (bl). 37 **Alamy Stock Photo:** Science Photo Library / Kateryna Kon (br). **Science Photo Library:** Dr Yorgos Nikas (tr). 40 **Alamy Stock Photo:** Classic Image (tl). **Dorling Kindersley:** The Science Museum, London (cl). 41 **Dreamstime.com:** Christianm (cr). **Science Photo Library:** (tr). 42 **Alamy Stock Photo:** F. Cortes-Cabanillas (cb); The History Collection (tl). 43 **Dreamstime.com:** Alexey Borodin (cr); Anat Chantrakool (cl); Sitthichai Kaewkam (c); Leisan Rakhimova (c/Ground tea). 44 **Wellcome Collection:** Edward Jenner. Oil painting. Public Domain Mark (tl). 45 **Dreamstime.com:** Eivaisla (cra). **Wellcome Collection:** Louis Pasteur. Photogravure. Attribution 4.0 International (CC BY 4.0) (tr). 46 **Alamy Stock Photo:** Artokoloro (cr); Matteo Omied (tl). 47 **Dorling Kindersley:** RGB Research Limited (tc). 48 **Alamy Stock Photo:** Historic Collection (tc); INTERFOTO / Personalities (c). **Getty Images / iStock:** E+ / gerenme (clb). 50 **Alamy Stock Photo:** Science History Images / Photo Researchers (tr); Sueddeutsche Zeitung Photo / Scherl (bc). **Science Photo Library:** Michael Abbey (bl). 51 **Alamy Stock Photo:** Imagebroker / Arco / Joko (crb). 52 **Alamy Stock Photo:** Pictorial Press Ltd (tl); Science History Images / Photo Researchers (cla). 53 **Alamy Stock Photo:** The Print Collector / Heritage Images (tl). **Science Photo Library:** Eye Of Science (cra); James Gathany (cr). 54 **Alamy Stock Photo:** INTERFOTO / Personalities (tl). 55 **Getty Images:** Hulton Archive / Print Collector (cb). **Wellcome Collection:** (br). 56 **Alamy Stock Photo:** Granger Historical Picture Archive, NYC (bl). 57 **123RF.com:** ballykdy (cra). **Dreamstime.com:** Witold Krasowski (bl); Waltercicchetti (fcra). 58 **Getty Images:** Stockbyte / C Squared Studios (bc). 59 **Alamy Stock Photo:** deefish (cra). **Dreamstime.com:** Stewart Behra (ca); Sierpniowka (br); Dphiman (bc). **Getty Images:** Stockbyte / David Bishop Inc. (tr). 60 **Alamy Stock Photo:** bildagentur-online.com / th-foto (cla); History and Art Collection (tr). **Science Photo Library:** Dr Kari Lounatmaa (bc). 61 **Division of Medicine and Science National Museum of American History, Smithsonian Institution:** (crb). 62 **Dreamstime.com:** Mykhailo Baidala (br); Beata Jana Filarova (bc). **Getty Images:** Science Photo Library / Wladimir Bulgar (cr); The Image Bank / Ian Logan (cl). 63 **Dorling Kindersley:** The Science Museum (bl). **Dreamstime.com:** Miloszbudzynski (cr). **Getty Images / iStock:** Coprid (cra). **Getty Images:** Science & Society Picture Library (tl); Science Photo Library / Wladimir Bulgar (br). 64 **Getty Images:** Mondadori Portfolio (tl). 65 **Alamy Stock Photo:** Travel USA (br). 66 **Getty Images:** SSPL / Science Museum (cb). **Science Photo Library:** Andrew Lambert Photography (bl). 67 **Alamy Stock Photo:** Science Photo Library / Kateryna Kon (crb). **Science Photo Library:** Corbin O'grady Studio (tr). 68 **Alamy Stock Photo:** Newscom / BJ Warnick (tl). **NASA:** JPL / Cornell University (cb). 69 **Alamy Stock Photo:** Newscom / BJ Warnick (crb). **Dreamstime.com:** Unteroffizier (tc). 70 **Dreamstime.com:** Artem Egorov (cb). **Getty Images:** French Select / Bertrand Rindoff Petroff (tr). 71 **Getty Images / iStock:** E+ / t_kimura (tr). 74 **Dorling Kindersley:** Science Museum, London (cb). **Dreamstime.com:** Georgios Kollidas (tl). 75 **Dorling Kindersley:** The Science Museum, London (clb). **Getty Images / iStock:** Stocktrek Images (tl). 76 **Alamy Stock Photo:** CPA Media Pte Ltd / Pictures From History (crb); IanDagnall Computing (bl). 77 **Dorling Kindersley:** Science Museum, London (cr). 78 **Alamy Stock Photo:** GL Archive (tl); Sueddeutsche Zeitung Photo / Scherl (cb). 79 **Getty Images:** Science & Society Picture Library (br). 80 **Alamy Stock Photo:** World History Archive (tl). 81 **Alamy Stock Photo:** Alliance Images (cr); Pascal Boegli (bc). **Getty Images:** Roger Viollet / Boyer (tr). 82 **Alamy Stock Photo:** IanDagnall Computing (tl). **Getty Images / iStock:** Ralf Geithe (clb). 83 **Science Photo Library:** Otis Historical Archives, National Museum Of Health And Medicine (br). 84 **Alamy Stock Photo:** Malcolm Haines (cra); Pictorial Press Ltd (tl). 86 **Getty Images:** Bettmann (tl). 87 **Hagströmer Medico-Historical Library, Karolinska Institutet:** (crb). **NASA:** (cr). 88 **Alamy Stock Photo:** VTR (bl). **Dreamstime.com:** Yodke67 (crb). 89 **Alamy Stock Photo:** PJF Military Collection (bc). **Getty Images:** Bettmann (clb). 90 **Dorling Kindersley:** The Science Museum (cla). **Getty Images:** Corbis Historical (tr); Hulton Archive / Apic (crb); Science & Society Picture Library (bl). 91 **Alamy Stock Photo:** ClassicStock / H. ARMSTRONG ROBERTS (tl); Chris Willson (crb); INTERFOTO / History (bc). **Dreamstime.com:** Axstokes (br); Cowardlion (tc). **Getty Images / iStock:** E+ / DSGpro (cra). 92 **Alamy Stock Photo:** Aviation one (cl). **Dreamstime.com:** David Lloyd (cla). 93 **NASA:** (tr). 94 **Alamy Stock Photo:** Science History Images / Photo Researchers (tl). 95 **Alamy Stock Photo:** Science History Images / Photo Researchers (tr). **National Science Foundation, USA:** Steven C. Buhneing (br). 96 **Getty Images:** Hulton Archive / John Byrne Cooke Estate (tl). 97 **NASA:** Chandra / CXC (bc). **Science Photo Library:** (cra); I. Andersson, Oxford Molecular Biophysics Laboratory (crb); DESY (br). 98 **NASA:** (bl). 99 **Alamy Stock Photo:** stock imagery (crb). **NASA:** Bob Nye (cra). 100 **Alamy Stock Photo:** Forance (ca); PA Images / Peter Byrne (tr). **Dreamstime.com:** Sergei Chaiko (bc); Andrei Dzemidzenka (br). 101 **Alamy Stock Photo:** Paulo Oliveira (cla). **Dreamstime.com:** Anteroxx (tr); Dmitry Vinogradov (ca/car); Olga Popova (clb); Anton Starikov (bc). **Getty Images / iStock:** orestegaspari (ca). 102 **Alamy Stock Photo:** Darling Archive (tl). 104 **Sau Lan Wu:** Jeff Miller, University of Wisconsin-Madison. (tr). 105 **Alamy Stock Photo:** ZUMA Press, Inc. / © George Grassie (cr). 106 **Getty Images:** French Select / Bertrand Rindoff Petroff (tl). 107 **Science Photo Library:** Gregoire Cirade (br). 111 **NASA:** JPL (cr). 112 **Alamy Stock Photo:** CPA Media Pte Ltd / Pictures From History (tl). **Dorling Kindersley:** Stephen Oliver (bl); Science Museum, London (cla). 113 **Getty Images / iStock:** pixhook (bl). 114 **Alamy Stock Photo:** FLHC 62 (tr). 115 **Alamy Stock Photo:** Granger Historical Picture Archive, NYC (tc); The Reading Room (bl). **Getty Images:** Gamma-Rapho / Jean-Michel COUREAU (cra). 116 **Alamy Stock Photo:** Science History Images / Photo Researchers (bl); World History Archive (tl). 117 **Alamy Stock Photo:** The History Collection (tr). 118 **Science Photo Library:** (tl). 120 **Alamy Stock Photo:** Sueddeutsche Zeitung Photo / Knorr + Hirth (bl). 121 **Alamy Stock Photo:** Pictorial Press Ltd (br). 122 **Alamy Stock Photo:** Daniel J. Cox (crb). **Getty Images:** Ernesto Burciaga / Omniphoto.com (bl). **NASA:** European Space Agency / Technical University of Denmark (cb); Kim Shiflett (tr). 123 **Alamy Stock Photo:** Xinhua (tr). **Dreamstime.com:** Andrey Armyagov (cla). **NASA:** (cb); Johns Hopkins Applied Physics Laboratory / Southwest Research Institute (tl); ESA, CFHT, CXO, M.J. Jee (University of California, Davis), and A. Mahdavi (San Francisco State University) (br). **Science Photo Library:** James King-Holmes (bl). 124 **Alamy Stock Photo:** Pictorial Press Ltd (clb); Science History Images / Photo Researchers (tl). **Science Photo Library:** Hale Observatories (bl). 125 **NASA:** (br). 126 **Alamy Stock Photo:** Science History Images / Photo Researchers (cla). 126-127 **NASA:** SDO (tc). 127 **Alamy Stock Photo:** Science History Images (cra). 128 **Alamy Stock Photo:** allOver images / TPH (b). 129 **Alamy Stock Photo:** World History Archive (br). 130 **Science Photo Library:** Jeremy Bishop (bl). 131 **Getty Images:** Moment Open / by Mike Lyvers (tr). 132 **Alamy Stock Photo:** Krzysztof Jakubczyk (clb); Ruby (tl); NASA Image Collection (bc). 133 **NASA:** Event Horizon Telescope Collaboration (tr). 134 **Alamy Stock Photo:** Erik Pendzich (tl). **Getty Images:** FOX Image Collection (cl). 135 **Alamy Stock Photo:** Eddie Toro (tl).

All other images © Dorling Kindersley
For further information see: www.dkimages.com